# POSTCARDS FROM THE ROAD

## *Stories*

Published by Pepys2000 Writing    *pepys2000.blogspot.com*

ISBN: 9780692484135
Library of Congress Control Number: 2015911046
Printed in the United States of America

Design & Layout by Rod Burton
Roderick C. Burton - Art & Design   *rcburton.com*

# POSTCARDS FROM THE ROAD

## *Stories*

**Richard Little**

Bellingham, Washington

*For Cherie, with whom all things are possible.*

# Table of Contents

We shall not cease from exploration ...
T. S. Eliot

# Prologue

Tales told by travelers are as old as human history. Marco Polo comes to mind. Before him, Chaucer reveled in the antics of folke longen to goon on pilgrimages. Why stop there? From the dawn of time, the Hebrew Bible tells of Abraham and Sarah setting out from Ur of the Chaldees. The children of Israel had interesting stories to tell when Moses parted a sea and led them through the desert. There are countless other examples, including an Odyssey.

Whether called by God or pure wanderlust, what happens along the way becomes part of our culture — from the epic to the everyday, from the universal to the personal. John Steinbeck, Bill Bryson, William Least Heat Moon, and John McPhee, to name heroes of mine in the genre, continue an ancient tradition.

Why the fascination? My guess is that these stories scratch an itch to take a break from reality and explore what's around the corner, what's over the next hill. What are those other folks and different places like? Maybe, who are we? What are *we* like? That itch was what prompted my wife Cherie and me to find out — to pack the car in the spring of 2014 and drive across America.

And this time we wouldn't have to cross the vast expanse of the country on a time schedule — pedal to the metal, fudging the speed limit, rest stops and truck stops or non-stops — hypnotized by the endless ribbon of Interstate fading into the distance? We'd done that before: changing jobs, going to college, moving back home, or trying to fit an ambitious annual vacation into too little time. Haven't we all. What if, instead, we could take our time? Smell morning coffee at a small town cafe instead of diesel exhaust. Take a slow road, destination uncertain. Turn off the car and wait for a wild turkey to cross the road. Meet the people, the history, and the character of places that we'd heard of — some real, some imagined.

Without presuming to emulate the honored writers mentioned above, I knew I'd feel remiss if I didn't record some events, scenes, and stories we encountered on a much-awaited road trip. Some of these have been posted elsewhere, and I've been flattered to learn that a reader or two has folded into an easy chair, plumped up a pillow, and enjoyed the wanderlust with us.

Come on along!

# 1

# US 50

On Saturday morning May 3rd in Grand Junction, Colorado, I awoke to bright sunlight arrowing through a gap in our motel room curtains and into my eyes. I tiptoed into my jeans and pulled a sweatshirt over my head, not disturbing Cherie who happily snoozed away, and took my barefoot self out to a cozy patio ringed with shade trees. Coffee and a Danish retrieved from the motel lobby, I sank into a rattan chair next to a table with a green and white umbrella and listened to finches and pine siskins skittering and chattering in the branches. It was ten o'clock.

I basked in the warmth and restored my soul. After the long drives of the previous two days, we needed a good night's rest.

For us, Grand Junction was our jumping-off place to cross the United States, starting on Highway 50, the self-described "Loneliest Road in America." The nickname came about as follows: The original east-west cross-country highway system consisted of two-lane roads through the middle of cities and towns for all of its 3,000 miles. The routes were numbered from the Dakotas south, US 10, 20, 30, et cetera. In 1956 President Eisenhower's National Interstate and Defense Highways Act set in motion the then-largest public works project in American history, eventually building the interstate highway system we know today. For the route of new Interstate 80, US 40, not 50, was chosen. I-80, beginning in San Francisco, now crosses the Sierra Nevada Range over Donner Pass (of immortal fame), skirts the north end of Lake Tahoe, and goes on through Reno to Salt Lake City, and beyond.

US 50, to the south, bisects the continental United States smack across its midsection. It likewise begins in San Francisco as before, travels through Sacramento, and summits Echo Pass before dipping down to Lake Tahoe. It then heads off into and across Nevada (Carson City, Ely), into and across Utah (Green River), and on to Colorado at Grand Junction. Eventually, US 50 visits St. Louis, crosses Illinois, Indiana, Ohio, West Virginia, and Virginia, and passes through downtown Washington D.C. on its way to Annapolis. It's not done yet. It completes its journey in Ocean City, Maryland.

From sea to shining sea!

It was this America we set out to explore — to visit small towns we'd never heard of, places "forgotten" when cross-country traffic dried up. Also destinations like "Ozarks" and "Blue Ridge" and "Mighty Mississippi" — names of places that make it into newspapers or on TV from time to time, slot into pre-determined sections of our brains, and then are stashed away.

So, ahead there would be stop signs and small town speed limits, farm trucks and hay trailers, two-lane roads and winding detours — *Blue Highways* in William Least Heat Moon's classic phrase, and Mom's Diners and Randy's Kitchens. Off we went on roads less traveled.

The narrative that follows does not begin in San Francisco or other points to the west, because we'd seen much of California, Nevada, and Utah on earlier travels. I grew up in Sacramento and spent the early years of my life on summer hikes and campouts in the Sierras and swims in Lake Tahoe. Since moving to Washington State, Cherie and I have taken several trips through the magnificent expanses of Nevada and Utah, part of the West's Great Basin.

The Great Basin was once an inland sea, the remnant of which is the Great Salt Lake. It extends from the Sierra

Nevada in the west to the Wasatch Mountains east of Salt Lake City; from southeastern Oregon and southern Idaho to Las Vegas. Despite some first impressions, it's amazing territory — "desolation," in the salutary sense of the word — consisting of vast distances, sparse population, monumental vistas, and profound silence. It is beautiful country, but we sped through just a corner of it. Our cross-country itinerary was about what lay from there eastward.

Our home, Bellingham, Washington, lies just below the 49th parallel north latitude, the border with Canada. Grand Junction is at 39° north latitude, roughly equivalent to Sacramento. The Pacific Coast is at 122° west longitude. Grand Junction in the western foothills of the Rockies is at 108°. Picture us, then, on a diagonal, the hypotenuse of a right triangle, 850 miles on one side and 930 miles on the other. Happily, I left square roots behind in high school, but it worked out to ten hours one day, twelve the next.

But for a mandatory stop at a Krispy Kreme in Issaquah, Washington, and a Happy Hour frappuccino in Pendleton, Oregon, that hit the spot in the 90-plus heat, there is nothing remarkable to report the first two days of high-speed travel — that is, until we reached Snowville, Utah, the day after a night's rest in Ontario, Oregon. And met Fiona.

There is no good place to run out of gas, is there? But

some are worse than others. A big city downtown intersection, perhaps. How about the desolation of the northern Utah desert?

South of Twin Falls, Idaho, a worried look at the gas gauge sent us to the owner's manual. Slowing down and coasting down grades would not get us to the next town of any size, Tremonton, home to around 8,000 folks. For the record, I take complete blame for this inauspicious beginning. Cars don't run on blame, do they?

Just then, arising out of the asphalt heat waves ahead loomed a mirage, a Flying J Travel Plaza sign. Next to it, another that announced "Mollie's Cafe." We were saved! And after gassing up, relieved and hungry.

Snowville, Utah, (pop. 169) is home to two businesses, period, as far as we could tell. One of them, Mollie's, was packed. Fiona the waitress could be a model, or a stand-up comedian. She was a prom princess, homecoming queen, student body president, carried a four-point, and got a full ride to Utah State in track. She's all of 26. "Mollie" is Fiona's grandmother, so to hell with sticking it out for two years of MBA prep. She came back home to run the restaurant. She loves it.

She handled the overflow lunch crowd with a smile — hungry road-travelers like us, families with kids, two old farts in the corner — and fended off raunchy comments from a table of regulars in coveralls wearing wide-brim cowboy hats, black or tan. They got a kick out of dropping phrases like "bull semen" when Fiona refilled their coffee. She was unfazed.

We sat at the counter. Shouting from behind a pass-through to the kitchen, the frazzled cook yelled at us, "I lie awake with nightmares about days like this!" Fiona laughed and asked if we needed more time with the menu. Her smile and witticisms, the wise-cracks and giggles, the speed with which she negotiated counter corners and tables and defeated a balky refrigerator door with one hand, refilling glasses and balancing full plates on her other arm should have been posted on YouTube.

We ordered lunch. Fiona took time to look at me over her notepad and wrinkle her nose over my choice of potato salad as a side order to my cheeseburger. I stuck to my guns and she sailed away, her green, unstained "Mollie's" t-shirt somehow still tucked into her jeans. The green matched her eyes. Her scuffed-up pink tennis shoes, on the other hand, told the tale of how hard she'd worked since before the breakfast shift. Before we left, she offered to knock ten percent off our check if we'd stay and do dishes. The food was great — including the potato salad.

Then we were off, and down through the fast, hellish speedway from Ogden to Provo with Salt Lake City in between, branching off finally on US 6 near Provo. The route travels through pretty canyons and past desert mesas southeast to Green River, Utah. The long twelve hours from Ontario to Grand Junction paid off — with a big assist by a fashionable and funny gal at a roadside diner in a speed-bump of a town in the high Utah desert called Snowville.

# 2

# On the Road

After showers and a satisfying breakfast in Grand Junction, we regained Highway 50 and drove toward the mountains, able to take our time now after two hard days on Interstates. The miles drifted by. So much solitude, even when accompanied. Cherie, who can't sleep in the car, dozed quietly, her head on a pillow against the passenger window. (We *always* take our pillows along, and so should you.)

Anyway, Cherie non-slept, and my mind, lulled by fence posts and sycamore trees lining the road and no traffic to speak of, drifted down familiar synapses. I calculated once again the elapsed time to a destination between driving 75 mph versus 60. (Hint: just reduce the time by one-fourth.) Do razor blade models I buy get less sharp over the years because Gillette plans obsolescence in order to bring out newer iterations? Other important stuff like contemplating the milliseconds after the Big Bang and what would a world without Velcro really be like. Same question re WD40.

In my reverie, I retraced a curious event a couple of days earlier — namely three arresting dining tableaux at a restaurant our first night out.

After turning east at Seattle, we'd summited the Cascades at Snoqualmie Pass, raced past Yakima ("The Palm Springs of Washington"), sped through the Yakima Valley, and turned south to cross the Columbia River. Ordinarily, scenery is not the chief attraction between Ellensburg, Washington, and the Tri-Cities, but this spring the foothills had a green fuzz on them and Mt. Adams and Mt. Rainier in the distance were white with snow.

After putting the day's Interstate behind us, we checked

into a motel in sadly forgettable Ontario, Oregon, tossed our luggage on the bed, and decided on the closest restaurant, one of the familiar national franchises at freeway interchanges that fasten themselves to equally common, well-advertised sleeping establishments. Tired, but not too tired to skip dinner, we crossed the asphalt parking lot and were seated at a vinyl and chrome booth and handed menus.

At once a voice rang out and I jumped.

"She's just so *negative*. All the time!" This came from a table two booths away from us where four people sat. The woman's voice was shrill and felt like thumbtacks attacking my eardrums. She might as well have been using a megaphone.

Her foursome was sipping apple-tinis — for dessert. The speaker's bleary-eyed husband sat beside her; the other couple was directly across, no more than three feet away.

The blaring went on. "The other day, it was her *husband*. Yesterday, it was *church*. Should have *seen* how she was dressed. And I won't even *start* about her hair. *Negative*, I tell you, *always* putting people down. Last week when it finally got sunny, she ...."

The server arrived, a pleasant young Latina with pretty hair, so I asked her why the woman was talking so loudly. She rolled her eyes, and gestured over her shoulder at the two men at a booth across the room as if to say You think *she's* bad?

We'd seen that interaction, too — two scowling grumps, one bald, the other with messy hair. One had growled, "Well, it's kinda too late now, now isn't it?" not deigning to look up at the nice young lady. Seems she'd delivered the wrong side dish. Horrors! However discomfited, the lapse hadn't stopped them from devouring their dinners and slurping coffee. They didn't speak or smile at one another.

The service was slow, but we had arrived just behind a large party. A group of ten was seated across the room from us. They crowded around a table beneath a sign pointing the way to the bar. Their voices had to carry to out-shout happy patrons down the hall from them.

"I haven't went back to the library since!" boasted one man. Since when, I wondered. Since they stocked up on all those *books*? *Grammar* books? There were John Deere hats on two good ole boys: overalls over a swimsuit top on a twenty-something girl with a stringy blonde ponytail, a tie-dyed t-shirt on her boyfriend who sported a skimpy goatee and wrapped a skinny arm around her shoulders. His dad, I assumed, was muscling food into his maw, and a very large, large mom was coaxing her ten-year old to eat. This was not da Vinci's *Last Supper*, but apparently it was supper in Ontario, Oregon, at the only three other occupied tables in a brand-name eatery a little after nine at night.

Then I caught myself. It dawned on me that this might be a teaching moment, an important aspect of the America we'd set out to see. Perhaps I'd better get used to folks who dressed and ate differently and don't talk Her Majesty's English so good. Maybe I'd better lighten up. We had a long road ahead.

The meal was tasty: liver and onions which I never get at home. No comment from Cherie. The loud, fingernail-on-a-blackboard woman and her hostages left. So did the sad old men, undoubtedly without leaving a tip. The contented family across the room lingered and laughed and tucked into dessert. Cake with candles; it was a birthday, song and all. We sang, too.

Before we finished dinner, I told the waitress that I'd last perhaps ten minutes doing her job, maybe less. She smiled as if she agreed. I hope I hadn't sounded condescending. We did leave a large tip, in cash, and left.

We slept well. The next morning before going down to breakfast, we popped some anti-Fox News meds just to be safe. In the complimentary eating area, the flat-screen sound was off, but I was able to lip-read while downing my cereal, hard-boiled egg, sweet roll, orange juice, and coffee. Sure enough, some dude in a suit with perfectly coiffed shiny hair and in black-rimmed glasses was saying that, once again, Obama lied.

We gassed up and put Ontario in the rear-view mirror.

It was a clear and sunny day. Bring on The Real America, however unlike the white-bread community in a relatively prosperous corner of the country where we lived. Wasn't this what we'd set out to see for ourselves?

We had set out with the usual apprehensions: Would the weather cooperate? Would people be friendly? Would the car behave? Would we cooperate, be friendly, behave?

Would folks see our late-model, expensive automobile with (gasp) far-off Washington State plates and have the same knee-jerk reaction that, admittedly, we might have to theirs?

A word about our conveyance. For a major birthday of Cherie's, one ending with a zero, we bought a new car. She'd been dutifully soldiering around town in a black, fifteen year-old pickup truck while I drove a utilitarian soccer-mom-red SUV. The excuse was the long travel I was frequently required to do and the better gas mileage the small car got.

Now, our vehicular home for thirty-five hundred miles across America, and mine for the thirty-five hundred mile return, was a late model "previously owned' vehicle. A black Audi, as it happens.

The car featured the usual bewildering array of bells and whistles seen in showrooms everywhere: seats (heated, if need be) which quietly whirred at the push of a button to adjust to each driver's posture, windshield wipers that automatically knew when it was raining and how hard, displays that kept track of real-time gas mileage, weather, compass direction, interior and exterior temperature, oil consumption, and for all I knew, important dates in history. The A/C and heating system had a brain and a dozen or so settings. The audio system was understandable to the average twelve year-old but beyond my ken.

Comfortable window seats reclined, there was plenty of leg-room and 360° visibility, nothing was stored in an overhead bin that might have shifted during take-off or landing, and the ample trunk held an ice chest full of beverages and nibblies. No endless check-in line, no baggage limit, no security screening or disrobing ("The belt, too, sir.") Not one noisy waiting room; no waiting, period.

On-demand rest stop breaks and no annoying passenger in the adjacent seat — speaking for myself at least. The car was a cinch to drive and got good mileage.

Only once was there a hiccup, but that story comes later. And it had more to do with me than the car.

As for other people we would encounter over thousands of miles and three weeks, I pledged an open mind. It was John Steinbeck's contention that

> For all our enormous geographic range,
> for all of our sectionalism, for all of our
> interwoven breeds drawn from every part of
> the ethnic world, we are a nation, a new breed.
> Americans are much more American than
> they are Northerners, Southerners, Westerners,
> or Easterners …. This is not patriotic whoop-
> de-doo; it is carefully observed fact ….
> Americans from all sections and of all racial
> extractions are more alike than the Welsh are
> like the English, the Lancashireman like the
> Cockney, or for that matter the Lowland Scot
> like the Highlander.

We had very little personal experience to know if this was true or not, particularly about the *terra incognita* we were heading to. But hopefully without sounding chauvinistic about it — and certainly to over-generalize — Steinbeck's observation sounded right. There's something to be said about a nation of immigrants, all of whose mothers and fathers had been seekers for something new, would have a certain openness and independence and much in common. I don't want to get ahead of myself, and again, we would find out.

23

# 3

# The Rockies

Grand Junction is a pleasant town at the confluence of the Gunnison and Colorado Rivers. It is a gateway to the wonders of southwest Colorado. The Uncompaghre Plateau rises off to the west. Enormous Grand Mesa is to the east, the largest flat-topped mountain in the world at 500 square miles, and looming 6,000 feet above the surrounding river valleys. I recalled an earlier slog to the top of the mesa some years ago in a 1980s passenger car in the lowest automatic transmission gear, foot to the floor, whizzing along at 20 mph, the vehicle gasping for oxygen.

This day, far off and ahead of us we could make out shapes of hazy mountains hinting at what lay ahead, a range several hundred miles wide, that the likes of John Frémont and others tried to tame. South and east of Grand Junction are the magnificent San Juan Mountains, home to many "Fourteeners." The term describes peaks higher than 14,000 feet, no fewer than fifty-three of which are in Colorado.

We stopped for excellent lattés at Moca Joe's [sic] in Montrose which the barista described as the "uniquest" town in Colorado.

She asked about our itinerary, and we got the first of many wide-eyed "Wows." Out of Montrose and due east, Highway 50 follows the Gunnison River. The Black Canyon of the Gunnison along the way is the result of two million years of carving by the river. It is 2,700 feet at its deepest and a few football fields wide at the rim. The view from the parking lot is *straight down*. The Gunnison River drops an average of thirty-four feet per mile through the canyon, compared to the seven and a half feet per mile the Colorado falls through the Grand Canyon.

Gunnison and the Black Canyon are named for Captain John Gunnison, explorer and surveyor of a transcontinental rail route in 1853. The town features rafting, camping, and other tourist amenities. For lunch, we chose the Gunnisack Cowboy Bistro recommended in a travel book. We ate a normal meal, unlike the group at the table next to ours where a foursome of healthy teenage boys ordered the Gunnisack's infamous dessert cookies. They made short order of enormous, plate-sized chocolate chip cookies mounded with ice cream and syrup. In spite of encouragement by a friendly waitress, we took a pass.

"Unique-est" is a perfect word to describe the Continental Divide. From the high desert of eastern Utah and western Colorado where we started — already more than a mile above sea level — the climb gets serious. Monarch Pass is one of the highest passes in a state that is famous for them. At 11,312 feet, it is over 500 feet higher than the summit of Mt. Baker back home, and we were on pavement!

Herewith, a digression into Rocky Mountain history.

John C. Frémont was either a gifted soldier and statesman, or a fool. A heroic explorer of the American West or a shameless self-promoter. Maybe all of the above.

"The Pathfinder," as he was dubbed:

(1) took control of California during the Mexican-American War (the Bear Flag Revolt in 1846) and proclaimed himself governor;

(2) for this he was charged with mutiny and

insubordination and court-martialed in 1847, only to have the charges reduced by President Polk;

(3) amassed a fortune in California before and during the Gold Rush, but nearly lost it all due to lawsuits by landowners he dispossessed; the Supreme Court eventually ruled in his favor;

(4) was the fledgling Republican Party's first candidate for President in 1856, losing to Democrat James Buchanan when the rival Know Nothing Party split off enough votes; and,

(5) died destitute in New York in 1890.

Along the way he was removed from his command (Department of the West) during the Civil War again for insubordination, a post to which Abraham Lincoln had appointed him; yet, in 1878 President Hayes made him governor of Arizona. The spelling of "Frémont" was an affectation.

You can't make this stuff up!

Why this all too brief summary of a remarkable if controversial life? Because on Day Three we were reminded of one of Frémont's more quixotic adventures.

Frémont, born in 1813, belonged to that tribe of humans who believe the laws of physics, including meteorology and of human nature, don't apply to their remarkable selves. At age twenty-eight, he enhanced his military and political chances by marrying Jessie Benton, adored daughter of the powerful Thomas Hart Benton, thirty-year senator from Missouri and principal exponent of Manifest Destiny. Over the years, Senator Benton had gone to extraordinary lengths to attack those who attempted to "mar the theater of John Charles Frémont," in one writer's words.

So it came to pass that after three fairly successful expeditions throughout the West (hence, "Pathfinder"), Frémont, at the encouragement of his father-in-law, decided to try to locate a suitable, more southerly, east-west passage through the Rockies. He undertook his Fourth Expedition into the Rockies, not least to enhance his reputation.

In 1848 he started west up the Arkansas River with thirty-five men — in the month of *October*. Even before setting out from Bent's Fort, then the westernmost outpost of the United States, he was strongly advised to abandon the idea. A foot of snow already lay on the ground. Ten thousand-foot mountains and higher lay ahead. Frémont hired a guide of questionable repute. The troop slogged on through bitter cold and blinding snow. The guide misdirected them. Animals died and so did members of the party. One day, it took Frémont's party an hour and a half to go 300 yards. This was enough for several of the men who voted to turn back. On December 22nd, the arrogant Colonel Frémont pressed on but eventually admitted defeat. By the time the remainder of his party staggered into Taos, New Mexico, he'd lost a third of his men.

We stopped and parked at Monarch Pass and in every direction we looked Frémont's foolhardiness was evident. Insurmountable mountains surrounded us, nearby and off into the immense distance. The snow still hadn't been completely cleared off the highway. The scene was breathtaking. This was May, not October, in a comfortable car, not on foot and no pack animals. We walked around a bit in the chilly air, then got back into the car and drove on.

From these lofty, thin-air heights, US 50 descends along the beautiful Arkansas River. The Arkansas rises in the Rockies, splashing and crashing and whirling downward for miles before leveling off and continuing its nineteen hundred-mile course east to the Mississippi. Southern Colorado is the land of important river headwaters. Besides the Arkansas, the Rio Grande rises not far to the north and the Colorado River begins on the opposite side of the Continental Divide.

The Arkansas River is a rafting mecca and the landscape is a geologist's dream: rock formations, roaring rivers, lakes, peaks and valleys, rapids and rafts, dinosaur quarries. Add fishermen, paddlers, outfitters, roadside vistas. Down the lush gorge we cruised and gawked.

Traveler Alert: Along the Arkansas River is Royal Gorge. We didn't stop. It's a theme park centered around a stomach-churning suspension bridge over a scary gorge 955 feet above the river below. Years ago, I threaded my way through a dusty parking lot past tour buses and crowds of tourists and found the ticket booth. It would cost $20 for the privilege of enjoying burro rides, wagon rides, a petting zoo, a wildlife park, a carousel, ice cream shop, and a gift shop ... and more! I think the zipline was extra. I decided I had better ways to spend money, turned around, and left.

This May, we emerged onto flat desert again, bypassed Pueblo, Colorado, and stopped in the town of La Junta (pronounced "La Hunta") for the night. We dined at a curious restaurant down a flight of stairs where, for the second night in a row, Cherie was served her beer in a bottle with her meal. No glass.

# 4

# Bent's Old Fort

In 1846 Susan Magoffin, eighteen years old and newly married, left Independence, Missouri, for Santa Fe (then in Mexico) along with her husband Samuel and his partner and older brother James. Susan and Samuel had been honeymooning in the East, but the enthusiastic young woman, a daughter of privilege from Kentucky, saw the prairie voyage to come as simply a continuation of her honeymoon. Brother-in-law James was by then a wealthy, experienced Santa Fe trader and a confidant of President Polk.

Historians are indebted to young Susan Magoffin because she kept a diary. Her entries throughout her journey, and extending to her time later in Santa Fe as a "belle," add wonderful and unexpected detail to what might otherwise be a dry recital of mountain passes, numbers of wagons and horses, ammunition, fortifications, and battles. She and Samuel arrived in July at Bent's Fort, on the Santa Fe Trail. Susan was several months pregnant.

Having read excerpts of Susan Magoffin's diary, and being fascinated anyway by accounts of exploration of the American West, stopping to visit Bent's Old Fort in Colorado was a must for us. The historic site is twenty miles northeast of La Junta, out in the middle of nowhere. We were not disappointed.

"The Great Migration," as it came to be called, was shifting into high gear in the spring of 1846. In one week that April, fifty-nine steamboats carrying six thousand passengers docked at St. Louis, from the upper Mississippi, from New Orleans, and from Ohio. Manifest Destiny was underway.

The Santa Fe Trail, established in 1821, joined St. Louis via Independence with the two hundred year old town of Santa Fe nearly a thousand miles away. 1846 was a "Year of Decision," according to historian Bernard DeVoto. Regardless of what Great Britain thought, Oregon was by then American territory; Mormons were about to set out on their trek to the Great Salt Lake; Mexico had become independent of Spain; and scores of trappers, explorers, and mountain men had returned east with stories that awakened people to the prospects of the endless expanse of the American West. Traders, adventurers, ne'er-do-wells, young families, prospectors, soldiers and soldiers of fortune, farmers, milliners, blacksmiths — all of them hopeful, most of them ignorant of the travails that lay ahead — left St. Louis for a better life.

In the early 1830s, brothers William and Charles Bent of St. Louis had seen the opportunity that lay ahead. In partnership with another businessman, Ceran St. Vrain, they built a trading post on the Santa Fe Trail. They chose a quiet bend on the Arkansas River and before long Bent's Fort was a hub of activity not only for trade but for further exploration. Ultimately it served a military purpose in the Mexican-American War. (The Alamo fell in 1836.) It was the only privately owned fortification in the West and the likes of Kit Carson, John C. Frémont, and Steven Watts Kearny made use of it as a rendezvous and home base.

To be sure, Susan Magoffin's life on the trail was eased somewhat by tables, cabinets, stools, and carpet in her conical tent. Her combs and mirror were at hand, as well as her Bible, her journal, and books. She slept on a camp bed with sheets, pillows, and counterpane. Her maid Jane had come along, too. She wrote in her journal of wild raspberries, gooseberries, and "plumbs" for dessert; of horrible heat and "vivid and forked lightning quickly succeeded by hoarse growling thunder." Heat so oppressive, she said, that "I had to pull all but my chemise off, and even that would have been sent off without regret had not modesty forbid me."

By the time Susan Magoffin arrived at Bent's Fort, however, she was not well. The carriage she rode in had crashed at a river crossing and she'd been knocked unconscious. Despite the care of a doctor, she went into early labor and lost her baby. She spent twenty days at Bent's Fort before her party continued on to Santa Fe. She convalesced in a spare but comfortable room.

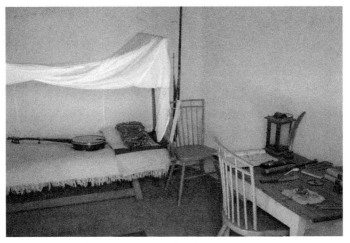

Susan Magoffin described life at Bent's Fort vividly, writing about "the greatest possible noise in the patio," horseshoing, children crying, servants quarrelling, Arapaho singing their chants. She wondered at painted Indians, watched Mexican ladies combing their hair in public and saturating it with grease, and remarked upon the uproar and confusion of troops.

Success at Bent's Fort as a trading post was one thing. More remarkably, for *fifteen years* the outpost was the scene of peaceful co-existence. William Bent maintained an enlightened relationship with the local Cheyenne. He married the chief's daughter and was adopted into the tribe. The fort bustled with daily activity among Mexicans, soldiers, trappers, Germans, French, Irish, and African-Americans, ranging from outfitting explorers, trading furs and manufactured goods, and entertaining guests in accustomed style.

Bernard DeVoto and others remark upon the Bents' inclusive relationship with Native Americans, but it was not to last. Manifest Destiny ran its tragic course. The fort burned down in 1849 under circumstances still unknown. William Bent later built a new fort farther east, but it is the "Old Fort" that captures the historian's imagination. The fort was meticulously restored, and designated as a National Landmark in 1976. Exact specifications had been prepared by an Army lieutenant in 1846 for defensive purposes during the Mexican-American War.

About the impending war and the preparations she witnessed, Susan Magoffin surprisingly wrote:

> The follies and wickedness of man! ...
> sinking himself to the level of the beasts,
> waging warfare with his fellow man even as
> the dumb brute ... striving for wealth, honour

and fame to the ruining of his soul and loosing
[*sic*] a brighter crown in the higher realms.

The peaceful, and according to some, duplicitous, surrender of Santa Fe to the Americans has been much recorded. Susan Magoffin's subsequent role in that former capital as a fine lady on a new American frontier, entertaining from her stately home, is a fascinating story of its own.

Our time at Bent's Old Fort was stirring. Stepping from room to room in a hands-on museum of early 19th Century Americana, we expected a mountaineer or prospector or Mexican trader to walk through the door and kick dust off his boots. A helpful docent in full regalia — slouch hat, blue-checked flannel shirt, red and white neckerchief, levis, sturdy belt, Jim Bowie knife — wandered here and there through the sparse crowd answering questions. Sitting in the shade beneath a balcony overhang, a Native American woman stitched a blanket. A pair of young people, volunteers or students or both, stoked a fire over which hung a black kettle. Add to this a brief introductory video and bookstore and a gift shop.

We walked back out through the sturdy wooden doors and back to our car. Colorado sky spread in all directions, the sleepy Arkansas River lazed along out beyond a copse of whispering cottonwood trees, and longhorn cattle kept drowsy watch in the warm sun.

Yes, I bought a t-shirt.

From Bent's Fort, we continued east on Highway 50 to Dodge City, Kansas.

# 5

# Gettin' Outta Dodge

Who could resist a visit to the iconic town of the Old West! Dodge City. *That* Dodge City.

Matt and Miss Kitty. And Chester and Doc. The Earps — Wyatt, and brothers James, Virgil, and Morgan. Bat Masterson and Doc Holliday. My childhood included lying in my bed on Sacramento nights listening to *The Lone Ranger* and *The Cisco Kid* on the radio. With the advent of TV, along with everyone else I moved on to *Gunsmoke* and *Maverick* and *Bonanza*, and all the others. Kit Carson, Jim Bowie, Daniel Boone, and Wild Bill Hickok were personal friends. On car trips past south Lake Tahoe, my dad could point out the exact spot where, backlit by pine trees and blue lake, Adam, Hoss, Little Joe, and Papa Ben rode toward us and into our living room.

Speaking of icons, I can conjure up Richard Boone and *Have Gun — Will Travel* in an instant and yes, even *Death Valley Days*. Extra credit if you knew that Burt Reynolds did a stint in *Gunsmoke*, as did Kelsey Grammer playing a character named "Frasier Crane"! News to me. How the West was Won is part of my heritage. For good, and in plenty of cases for bad, the American fascination with "The West," its reality and its myths, continues.

Here's our reality as we approached Dodge City, still on US 50 and following the Arkansas River. The heat that had been pleasant at Bent's Fort had moved the needle into uncomfortable. Tornado warnings we'd shrugged off a day earlier didn't seem as harmless as before. We whistled past the graveyard, trusting that Weather Channel wonks often overplay the meteorological mayhem they predict. For the first time, we rolled up the windows and surrendered to air conditioning, Northwesterners that we are.

But the heat assault was nothing compared to the visual one — a remarkable change from the faithful history of Bent's Fort.

Well before the affront to history Dodge was soon to offer, a chain store/fast food/gas station/big box/lowest common denominator corporate Americana display blazoned forth for miles on billboard after hand-made sign after billboard on both sides of the road.

Dodge City's commercial welcome far exceeded similar huckstering overload in other cities we'd seen or would see. Here's a partial list:

| | | |
|---|---|---|
| Amoco | Sam's Club | J.C. Penney |
| ARCO | Tacos Jalisco | Lotus Gardens |
| BP | El Torrito | Subway |
| Chevron | Union 76 | Godfather's |
| Safeway | La Quinta | King Buffet |
| Sam's Club | Best Western | Long John Silver's |
| Sears | Boot Hill Bed | Kohl's |
| Staples | & Breakfast | Kroger |
| Target | Days Inn | Lowe's |
| Taco Time | Sinclair | Macy's |
| Taco Bell | Gunsmoke Travel Park | Casey's Cowtown |
| Casa Alvarez | TownePlace Suites | Central Station |
| Conoco | Dodge House Hotel | Hong Kong |
| Exxon | Montana Mike's | Lotus Garden |
| Holiday Inn Express | Applebee's | Golden House |
| Thunderbird Motel | Bella Italia | Sarocha's Thai |
| Comfort Inn | Sunoco | Office Depot |
| Super 8 | Texaco | Office Max |
| Sonic | Valero | Petco |
| Arby's | Ace Hardware | PetSmart |
| Burger King | Albertsons | Pier 1 |
| McDonald's | AutoZone | Ross |
| Pizza Hut | Barnes & Noble | Taqueria Mexicana |
| Irving OIl | Bed Bath & Beyond | Tres Amigos |
| Marathon | Best Buy | El Charro |
| Mobil | KFC | Taco Palente |
| Phillips 66 | Cabela's | Paleteria |
| Shell | Costco | Rio Grande |
| TJ Maxx | Crate & Barrel | ...and don't forget |
| Toys "R" Us | Dick's Sporting Goods | IHOP |
| Wal-Mart | The Home Depot | |

I do not exaggerate. I took notes while Cherie drove. I wish I'd filmed it. American commercialism — tacky, trashy, cheap, gluttonous, ugly, shameless, and pandering. I offered up a silent prayer of thanks to Lady Bird Johnson whose Highway Beautification Act of 1965 curbed most of such excesses along the Interstate system.

Perhaps it's unfair to single out Dodge City after all. Lots of cities across the country are offensive in this way. What made it worse in Dodge was the disconnect between the advertising on steroids we encountered and what I'd hoped to feel. "Old Dodge" was not there; the broadcast collection of franchise motels, gas stations, eateries, and megastores was.

The main street through town, Wyatt Earp Avenue, of course, was busy, car-congested, and frighteningly hot. Would there be *any* commemoration of history? Turns out there was, sort of. Paralleling Wyatt Earp for a few blocks to our left was what looked like a badly worn-out Western movie set. Maybe it *was* a former movie set. Facing passersby was an array of storefronts — faux blacksmith shop, a shoddy saloon, cheesy trinket and t-shirt shops — cheek-by-jowl, each unattractive in its own way.

I looked for redemption. A steely-eyed gunslinger slapping

a silver dollar down on the bar and sauntering out of the saloon into the hot street at high noon to face down an unshaven and dirty-faced bad guy in greasy chaps and open-necked black shirt whose sweaty and shaky gun hand hovered over his holster. Gary Cooper staring down Lee van Cleef. One of them would soon be sprawled in the dust, and we onlookers, hiding in safety behind hitching posts and water troughs and louvered swinging saloon doors but unable to look away, knew which one it would be.

Alas.

The closest we came to the confrontational staple of the Wild West was when we did pull over and stop. We parked in front of a gift shop picked at random. I had to see this close up; Cherie chose to stay in the car. I got out and went in through swinging doors. It was no cooler inside and was stuffed to the gills with paraphernalia. I browsed. A wristlet of "genuine" Indian beadwork caught my eye. I looked it over. It was plastic and looked like a local Girl Scout project; either that or it was from a place farther west than Dodge, say, China.

In my imagination I asked the woman behind the counter wearing a faded gingham dress if this was really all the better Dodge City could do. I phrased it more nicely than that, but she got my meaning. She gave me the evil eye. A scowl replaced her ersatz customer-service smile. I watched with alarm as she slowly reached under the counter and fumbled around for something. It sounded heavy and went "clunk." I started backing away. She didn't take her eyes off me. With a jerk of her arm, she pulled out … not her Colt `45, but a packet of Chamber of Commerce brochures in a wire metal caddy. She slapped it on the counter, extracted one, wrinkled and dusty, and handed it to me.

I snapped out of the reverie. She and her fellow merchants were only trying to make a dime in a lousy economy on a forgotten stretch of US highway. I thanked the lady and went out into the heat where sat our shiny, late-model expensive car with out-of-state plates. Next to it, with a primer-gray front fender, was an '84 Buick Skylark with probably 250,000 miles on it.

I showed Cherie the wristlet. $6.95. Our 4 year-old grandniece would like it. On the way out of town we saw a sign pointing the way to Boot Hill. We skipped it, nor did we try to find the Long Branch Saloon. We did drop some coin at a car-jammed McDonalds, then got outta Dodge.

At first we regretted having wasted time, but that's not being fair. We were all about seeing America after all — as adults. Tarnished childhood memories from TV and late-night radio could be reclaimed, but it might take awhile.

# 6

# Cherokee Bottoms, The Ozarks, and Throwed Rolls

The sun rises in the east and sets in the west. Eastward turns the globe. True, some Tea Partiers argue that a heliocentric solar system is only a theory. If so, it's a 450 year-old theory, reinforced by a moon landing or two.

And regardless of one's planetary theory, there's no arguing that driving eastward against the sun shortened our days and lost us an hour every so often as time zones were crossed. We'd begun to realize that we hadn't given ourselves enough time to stop and see *and* make forward progress. This became evident on only the fifth day of our expedition as we crossed the expanse of the great state of Kansas and into Missouri.

Our route east from Dodge City took us farther along the Santa Fe Trail. Despite its fabled flatness, Kansas was lovely. We didn't think it boring at all. Open fields and skies recalled Whitman's praise:

> The prairie-grass dividing, its special odor breathing ...
>
> ... of the open atmosphere, coarse, sunlit, fresh, nutritious ...
>
> *The Prairie-Grass Dividing*

We stopped that night in the town of Great Bend, Kansas.

Great Bend is so named because it lies at the northernmost bend of the Arkansas River (pron. "Ar-kanz-as," please) before it turns southeast into Oklahoma. Geography buffs will be interested to know that Great Bend, a town of 16,000, is two hours south of Lebanon, Kansas, the omphalos of the continental US. Kinsley, Kansas, which we passed through, calls itself "Midway USA." It's 1,561 miles from San Francisco and New York City, respectively. The weather was still stifling, temperature in the high 90s the afternoon we arrived. The TV continued to report tornado watches.

By the following morning the temperature had abated somewhat. We were in Great Bend to visit Cherokee Bottoms, just north of town, one of the country's outstanding bird refuges. It is estimated that *forty-five percent* of the millions of birds that migrate north or south through the United States land and forage at this 41,000-acre natural sink. Extensive ponds including the largest freshwater marsh in the US, many acres in size, are enclosed by half a dozen barely improved dirt roads atop earthen dikes. Access to some areas is restricted entirely.

We inched along, binoculars and camera at the ready. At every flutter and rustle, I hit the brakes. Things got interesting when we got to the larger expanse of ponds. A large pterodactyl swooped up out of the reeds and crossed the road in front of us. "Wow," we rookies shouted, certain we'd spotted a rarity.

We had barely opened our half-century-old *Peterson's Western Birds* when our amateurism was exposed. White-faced egret number one (clearly no *rara avis*) was followed by a flock of twelve or twenty. Despite the name, they were stark black. The white face was a patch visible only on the mounted exhibit behind glass at the visitor center. More flocks flew by later.

We saw snowy egrets, Eastern grosbeaks, many red-winged blackbirds, yellow-headed blackbirds, avocets, a Wilson's phalarope, a northern shoveler, ducks beyond counting or identifying, a harrier hovering hopefully in the air over a mid-morning snack, meadowlarks, confusing sandpipers and killdeer. We stopped trying to keep track. The dike road made a large rectangular circle and we took our time. Our favorite find was a pink-legged blacknecked stilt.

Over 320 species can be found in Cherokee Bottoms. Obviously, we missed a few, as the excellent, modern visitor center revealed. Tastefully displayed in exhibits behind glass were native fauna, avian and otherwise. Dozens of critters were perched on branches or dabbling in water or winging overhead or peeking out of reeds. There was an endless selection of books, so of course we bought one, namely about *eastern* birds. Into the trunk went my dog-eared *Peterson's*.

Behind us, outside beyond a lengthy floor to ceiling wall of glass, were the grass and flatlands and ponds of the Bottoms

— a plate glass barrier, our friendly attendant told us, behind which she watched an oncoming tornado the previous year. She tossed off this tidbit with the accustomed nonchalance of a native Kansan, Dorothy Gale to the contrary notwithstanding.

Regarding such meteorological vagaries — in particular the recent years of "drouth" that had shrunk many of the ponds — a garrulous regular interrupted and set us straight. In beater straw hat, overalls, and wizened hands the size of cantaloupes our interlocutor volunteered, repeatedly, that this was due to Mother Nature. "Mother Nature" (*Nay*-churr), he said, looking us in the eye and sweeping this arm pointing outside. I chose not to mention that Mother Nature also included her two-legged denizens with opposing thumbs who pump untold tons of $CO_2$ into the atmosphere daily. I was a guest.

And, we had to get on the road.

At a DQ back in Great Bend we enjoyed a mid-morning hot weather reprieve (Oreo blizzards) to the accompaniment of two giggly, ear-budded teenage girls in the next booth right out of central casting. Then east and south we drove, now on US 56 in the general direction of Wichita where, after a few miles, the Santa Fe Trail left us to continue its historic path northeast to St. Louis. Past the outskirts of Wichita, the route took us due east toward Missouri — not before, however, a friendly attendant at a Sam's Club gas pump island loaned us her membership card to fill up. It looked to be the last chance for fuel for awhile.

Washington State?" she said, eyeing the plates. "I have a cousin who moved to Tacoma. Where you headed?"

We told her about our itinerary and got the same "Wow" we got everywhere. We drove off, she waved, and we remarked again on how nice and helpful 99.99% of people are.

Across the Missouri border, we stopped for the night in the town of Nevada — that's *Na-vay-da*. Nevada has its own unique history, as so many towns do. Civil War buffs and those who didn't sleep through American History know the story of "Bleeding Kansas."

46

The Kansas-Nebraska Act of 1854 — another compromise along the way to the Civil War (see, Missouri Compromise of 1820, or the Constitutional Convention for that matter) — punted on the issue of slavery and left the decision to the voters in the two states. Bad idea. Pro-slavery Missourians and others, abetted by President Franklin Pierce's waffling, poured into Kansas to vote. So did anti-slavery partisans from the North. Massacres ensued, often between residents of the same town. One such town was Nevada.

Anti-slavery "Jayhawkers" ravaged Missouri border counties. Pro-slavery "Bushwhackers," claimed Nevada as the "Bushwhacker Capital" for its strategic position. Notables in the struggle included John Brown (abolitionist) and Frank James (brother of Jesse) who later in the Civil War was a Confederate soldier and outlaw. Kansas continued to bleed up to and during the war.

Present-day Nevada belies that sad chapter in U.S. history with its sleepy streets and the usual to-and-fro of shoppers and walkers. The motel was one of the nicest we'd found. Dinner was quite pleasant, despite the fellow in the bar who, without a clue what "Cinqo de Mayo" meant, didn't stint on his celebratory alcoholic intake.

We set out the next morning for the Ozarks.

The change from the pleasant rolling green hills of Kansas to the hillier and more treed Missouri was pronounced — as was the transition to "The South." The menus changed, for one thing. Over the ensuing days, we ate biscuits and gravy, fried chicken (for breakfast!), sweet potato pancakes, barbecued ribs, biscuits, southern fried chicken, grits and honey, sausage, gravy, and biscuits, throwed rolls (more about them later), flower pot rolls, glazed pork chops, black-eyed peas, corn bread … and have I mentioned biscuits?

Our objective in Missouri was to see firsthand the Ozarks. Forget the unfair derisive cultural descriptor, the Ozarks are a remarkable geological phenomenon — an elevated plateau encompassing much of southeast Missouri and parts of Arkansas. Wonderful mountains and rivers, craggy bluffs, and forests of hardwood trees: hawthorn, hickory, oak, chestnut, maple, pecan, sycamore, and hundreds of other species as far as the eye can see.

In south-central Missouri, amid patches of the Mark Twain National Forest, is the Ozark National Scenic Riverway. The Riverway is the only one of its kind in the country. Along the Current and Jacks Fork Rivers and past their confluence near the town of Eminence, the Federal government has set aside 134 miles of parkway — riverine parkway, seldom as much as a mile wide. Campsites are rudimentary. Canoeists, floaters, swimmers, fishermen, and birders can enjoy a paradise. So, unfortunately, do insects which didn't waste much time feasting on our succulent Northwest flesh — midges, gnats, no-see-ums, mosquitoes, and yellow jackets.

We surrendered quickly. Not so a mom and three kids who, in shorts and short sleeve shirts hopped out of their car and set off down a riverside trail. They had to have slathered themselves with industrial-strength insect repellent, probably outlawed by the EPA. Perhaps not. After a few quick photos, we were back in the car and along a forest service road to enjoy the truly beautiful scenery in air conditioned comfort. Next time, on with the "Off" at the very least.

Our stop for the night was the town of Miner, Missouri. We arrived later in the day than we'd planned and we were hungry. The motel where we stayed was ho-hum but Lambert's Cafe down the street was, well ....

We were not prepared for Lambert's. You can't prepare yourself for your first visit to Lambert's, home of "Throwed Rolls." The place defies adequate description, but here goes.

The entryway was unassuming enough, but we rounded a corner and stopped and stared at an over-the-top eclectic, jammed, noisy, flavorful dining room and diners — an eatery the likes of which neither of us had ever seen. The room was the size of a very large school cafeteria or an airplane hangar. This was only one of *two* rooms, each crowded with an enormous sea of tables — benches actually, back to back, with the tables in between — patrolled by smartly dressed servers dishing out "pass-arounds." These were complementary side dishes, ready or not — roasted potatoes and onions, black-eyed peas, macaroni and tomatoes, fried okra, and fresh apple sauce.

But the star of the show was the deadly accurate flinger of the signature "throwed rolls." He wandered the aisles pushing a cart loaded with piping hot rolls fresh from the oven, loudly hawking his wares. Hollerin' "throwed rolls," he'd hurl one with deadly accuracy to someone who raised a hand across the cavernous room or flip one to a kid at a nearby table. Drop one, and he'd throw another.

The story goes that in 1942 Earl and Agnes Lambert with 14 cents between them borrowed $1500, hired five employees, and opened a restaurant. There were nine stools at the counter and eight tables. There was a World War on and meat and other provisions were rationed, but legendary good cooking soon trumped all difficulties — down-home delicious cookin' off of the menu, supplemented by pass-arounds and throwed rolls. A million license plates now cover the walls, state flags hang from the ceiling over the heads of the host of diners by the dozen. No liquor is served.

The food was delicious. It just kept coming. From the menu, corn off the cob, cole slaw, cooked carrots, baked potato, turnip greens, sliced peaches, candied yams, and mashed potatoes, all of them side-dishes to accompany barbecued chicken, chicken fried steak, chicken pot pie, chicken and dumplings, meatloaf, roast beef, ribeye, ribs, catfish, shrimp, ham steak, pork chops, hog jowl (which I ruled out), and frog's legs (ditto).

Our gentlemanly waiter confessed he'd made a mistake not getting our fried chicken order in promptly, ahead of a busload of hungry travelers. He atoned by bringing more and more pieces until we begged him to stop. Dessert? Forget it! We staggered out. Lambert's. Not to be missed.

Next day, the Mighty Mississippi.

# 7

# **The Bee**

Before telling about crossing the Big River, the unwelcome exposure to insects in the Ozarks was in fact the second event of its type on our way.

There are things you learn about each other on a venture such as the one we took. Not necessarily new things, but character quirks that are brought into more visible relief over long hours in X cubic feet of enforced confinement. We all know this as we weigh whether or not to travel with a companion no matter how good a friend he or she may be.

Cherie and I have enjoyed a long and happy marriage — two kids, two careers, two home remodels, wallpapering. But now, in early retirement and in each other's company more often, perhaps feelings that hibernate below the surface might percolate to the top through mile after mile of silence on this the longest road trip we'd undertaken. We travel well together as a rule, but over the years we've also enjoyed solitary time. Made a point of it, in fact. Put simply, we're independent people who love each other. We make joint decisions; unless we don't. My beautiful wife's patience is legendary; I work at it. Driving directions, map queries, restaurant and motel choices, potty stops might be fertile ground for disagreement. Nothing as routine as that happened, but there were some surprises.

I knew Cherie hated bugs — from the most harmless of moths and gangly crane flies to the B-52 houseflies that thrive in the Northwest. Don't even start about spiders. If an arachnid had been the subject of this brief episode, I likely would not be here to write about it. Her tolerance for flying critters is close to nonexistent. (The six-legged variety, that is; she is a bird-lover.)

She comes by her aversion honestly: Cherie grew up on the East Coast where some insects are the size of small birds — cockroaches in particular, ugly huge, Carboniferous Era, corner-lurking, night-crawling omnivores. Bad enough that they roam around in the dark, snacking on smudges of left-over pizza stuck to the box. When the overhead light flashes on, the miscreants scatter, skittering into nooks and crannies too small for you to get at. Sometimes as you sneak up on one with a rolled-up newspaper to send it to the lower reaches of Hell, you find out it can also fly! At you!

I'm not fond of the little beasties either, even if West Coast roaches are smaller and in my experience not as plentiful. For sure there's an important place for cockroaches in the ecosystem. There's probably a Save The Roaches society somewhere — t-shirts, monthly meetings, marches on Black Flag headquarters. The Franz Kafka Chapter in downtown Manhattan, perhaps.

Neither variety of these vermin, however, is the subject of this narrative. Rather, members of the wonderful entomological order *hymenoptera*, consisting of bees, wasps, yellow jackets, and hornets. These industrious denizens of spring, summer and fall perform wonders. Colonies live in beautifully constructed villages with intricate passages. They protect and pay homage to a monarch, provide childcare, guards and workers, and roam far and wide to find food, yet make their way home. They band together and defend against enemies. Bees even provide us food, however grudgingly.

But they sting. Or bite.

Like the one that flew in the driver's-side window, Cherie at the wheel, narrowly missing her head before disappearing somewhere in the car. There aren't a lot of options when this happens in a vehicle traveling 75 miles per hour. Skilled driver that she is — and screaming like she'd been shot — Cherie came as close as she's likely to come to a NASCAR sideways drift and pulled into a fortuitously wide driveway and jammed the brake.

Where was the bee? Or wasp. Whatever. "It flew down there," she yelled, pointing down beside her left leg, where, probably dazed by its collision with the window post, it was coming to its senses and assessing the wide cuff opening of Cherie's slacks. Out the door she flew as fast as her tormentor had flown in.

Am I making too much of this drama? My wife sure as hell didn't think so. "So do something," she yelled from a good fifteen feet away.

I got out of the car, stretched, and walked around the front. It was a bright sunny Utah afternoon, brown desert scrub to one side, distant green foothills in the other. At the end of the curving driveway sat a smallish pair of buildings surrounded by a chain-link fence. Then I noticed the sign. The Carbon County Humane Society! Terrific! I would commit brutal insecticide of one of God's elegant creations whose only mistake it was to fly at an inopportune moment through airspace it had far more right to than we did — in front of a Humane Society.

Maybe I wouldn't find him. Maybe he, or she, had expired. Maybe … nope, there it was, crawling its sextipedal way over the door jamb. From whence it harmlessly flew away without so much as a fare-thee-well.

Am I overstating the drama? Man versus beast, if not exactly grizzlies in Yellowstone? I'll let the reader ask my wife who shakily resumed her place behind the wheel and drove on, while I resumed my place in the reclined passenger seat and fell back asleep.

At this point, fairness compels me to add, speaking of character tics (not ticks!) that become more noticeable over time, I snore. "Vigorously," it must be said. But Cherie didn't say a word about that over thousands of miles.

# 8

# The Big Muddy

There are only three places left in the US to truly channel your "Huck n' Tom" and cross the Mississippi River by water. Not on a raft exactly, but on a ferry in the far southeast corner of Missouri. The unincorporated community of Dorena sits on the panhandle that looks on the map like a boot heel. The Dorena-Hickman Ferry is owned and operated by the Mississippi County, Missouri, Port Authority, established 1996. It crosses to Hickman, Kentucky.

Finding the ferry landing was an adventure of its own. The tiny black lines on the map were little help; same with non-existent roadside signs saying "Mississippi River This Way." We navigated by dead-reckoning and by guess and by golly. Out in the middle of nowhere on a two-lane road, we followed fence lines through endless fields of crops. Lush soybean fields and rows of new corn stretched in all directions broken up here and there by windbreaks — cottonwood, hickory, and pine.

"You sure?" we asked each other more than once.

"It's got to be somewhere," I said to myself as much as to my indulgent passenger. "There *is* a ferry. Google and the map both say so."

On and on, in a continual-loop dream of agricultural greenness, we drove — left turn, straight-away, right turn, around a curve, more straight road ahead — and with no way to get our bearings. Finally, we braked hard at a small sign to Dorena, a black arrow that pointed left. We pulled over. A tiny scratch mark on the map went *past* Dorena to the river! To turn or not? We crossed our fingers and plunged ahead. There had to be the river.

*Yes!*

We turned a final corner, drove a hundred yards, and dead-ended at the Mississippi. No toll booth, no welcome, no nothing. Just us and thousands and thousands of swimming pools-full of brown, muddy moving water where the asphalt ended.

In truth there were two signs: the familiar octagonal red-and-white one you could argue was unnecessary, and another small sign on a pole that said "Wait here for ferry." On the other side of the pole there was a small device: "Push button for ferry." The small black button stuck out of a gray plate the size of an off/on light switch. I pushed it. It made no sound. Back in the car, we waited, and we waited.

A utility truck pulled in behind us. I walked back to talk to the driver.

He smiled, "Y'all from Washington, huh?"

"Yes sir. Say, do you know if ...."

"I been there once-t. Stationed in Bremerton. Beautiful place."

"So's Missouri. Do you use this ferry a lot?"

A friendly smile acknowledged my furrowed brow. He allowed that some days the river was too rough. Was today one of those days? Can't tell yet was his reply.

Terrific. We'd gone miles out of our way. Backtrack?

"How will we know?"

"We just wait awhile. Where y'all been?"

I told him our itinerary and got the same reaction everyone had along the way: Wow!

A pick-up truck arrived. A "Show Me Stater" got out, took one look at the current, and got back in his truck and left.

"Not to worry," said my new best friend. "He lives around here. Just curious."

We chatted some more to kill time. Nice man. I took a stroll among the riverside trees and listened for birds. Cherie read a tour book. The truck's horn beeped.

There across the river, chugging resolutely up the mighty big water, was a tiny ferry boat. The current *was* strong, much faster than I'd have guessed given how far south we were. The unimaginable push of so many tons of river, so wide, so fast — this was the Father of Waters, indeed. Wavelets broke on the sand at my feet.

The boat looked like it wasn't getting any closer. It stayed the same size from our vantage point, but we could see it was walking its way up the river sideways until it could make its way directly to our shore. The pilot had done this before.

The boat docked, dropped its ramp, and off drove a passenger car and a haying tractor. Fourteen dollars later, we

were loaded and ready to cast off. Dorena is as far downriver from St. Louis as Hannibal is north — Sam Clemens' boyhood town. As if on cue, down from the cabin came Huckleberry Finn, himself — a better-dressed Huck, but a pretty good approximation of a boyhood hero.

Only as an adult have I learned that *Huckleberry Finn* is an "important book." As a boy lying on the grass in my backyard, that book and *Tom Sawyer* were escapist fantasies in every sense of the word. Who didn't fall in love (or lust) with Becky Thatcher exploring that cave with Tom? Who didn't have a clueless neighbor kid who could be conned into painting a fence or mowing the lawn? And who didn't have a raft?

In fact, I did. I built a Kon Tiki on our backyard swing set, testing not only the weight-bearing capacity of scrounged lumber but my sweet mother's patience. I put a tent on top of the plywood deck and rafted the Pacific with Thor Heyerdahl. I star-gazed at night. There was even a "bad boy" down the street who I played with from time to time who was unconcerned about rules and consequences and of whom my mother strongly disapproved.

Here in real life was our Huck — straw hat, studied nonchalance, tan face, and mischievous grin. The vape he casually held in his hand and took hits on was as out-of-bounds in Missouri that day as Huck's corncob pipe was a century and a half ago.

We told him about our trip. He flirted with Cherie. He asked if he could come along, but on second thought, he'd have to decide which of his three girlfriends to bring, only two of whom knew about each other.

He posed for a photo, not for the first time I'm sure.

Tough duty, sailor!

The ferry's motor came to life and we were off. The waves bumped, the boat rumbled, and we braced against the wind and the current's chop. Now, actually afloat on it, once again the size and brawn of the biggest river in America was sobering. Facing north upriver and holding on as we crossed was one of those breath-stopping times when the immensity of the country's history and the natural forces that shaped it became indelible. The river had been here down the ages, and petty men like us, to paraphrase Shakespeare, could only look about at it and stand in awe.

In less than an hour we docked and disembarked. I'd

channeled Mark Twain, albeit to the throb of diesel. What a life his must have been!

We pointed the car toward Grand Rivers, Kentucky, where we'd spend the night — yet another place we'd never heard of.

We prayed it would be cooler.

# 9

# Pokey's Cafe

You wouldn't give Pokey's Cafe more than a sidelong glance as you drove by. Neither did we. It happened, however, to be across the street from the Grand Rivers Inn where we arrived the afternoon of May 7th.

"Inn" was a bit much — it was a motel — but the proprietor was friendly and the place was clean, nicely if modestly furnished, and it showed the caring touches of its owner, Veronika, a Hungarian émigré of many years standing. Veronika was a pleasant-looking woman in her fifties, I'd say, with blonde hair cut short. She wore a sensible khaki-colored skirt and a white sleeveless blouse. Her sandals were orange with tan rope straps. She checked us in, made sure we were satisfied, and put the keys on a nightstand.

It was still hot, hot, hot and humid when we checked in. The thermometer had hit 98 the day before in Kansas and there were still tornado watches scattered around the Midwest. We turned on the A/C full-bore, collapsed on the bed, slept, and tried to fend off heat exhaustion.

We would not have crossed the street to Pokey's had not

Veronika told us there was a commercial washer and dryer on the premises. After naps, over we trudged through the damnable heat loaded down with a week's worth of laundry.

Pokey's is another roadside attraction, to borrow a Tom Robbins title. It's painted entirely in a distinctive red and undoubtedly had once been a service station. The words "Pokey's Cafe" and "Live Bait" are scrawled large in white cursive on signboards attached to the building; so is the announcement "Golf Cart Rental." Down the street and across is a car wash, a gas station, an ice machine, soft-serve ice cream and burger joint, a realtor, other unremarkable buildings, and a quote "resort" unquote. In other words, Anywhere USA.

The primary commerce of Pokey's appeared to be the bait shop which, through the door beneath that legend, we entered and were greeted by Larry, the man in charge. Larry, fortyish, had on worn trousers and a light blue workman's shirt with the sleeves rolled up. His hair was in a disarray that may have been intentional given his usual clientele. He couldn't have been nicer as he led the way to the washer and dryer in a small room in the back.

The word "Grand" as applied to the modest, small community we were in seemed, well, grand. But the size of the town that time of year was deceiving; fishing season had not started. When it did, Pokey's would be a gold mine. The bait shop was a crowded but orderly swarm of supplies: box after box after shelf after aisle of every bit of paraphernalia imaginable — lures, hooks, flies, rods, reels, line, sinkers, bobbers, salmon eggs, tackle boxes, creels, boots and waders, floats, nets, minnow buckets, hand pumps, oars, vests, gloves, insect repellant, sunscreen, lamps, flashlights and batteries, electronic fish finders. Once the season began, Larry'd offer live bait in the back as advertised. If it existed, Larry had it in stock.

The surprise was in the next room as we followed Larry's lead. As if he were expecting family for dinner, there was his neat and tidy restaurant. Tables were carefully set with attractive place mats and silverware, salt and pepper shakers, and napkin dispensers. At each table was an eclectic selection of comfy chairs. A chalkboard on the wall advertised the choices for breakfast: bacon, sausage, or ham and two kinds of toast. The eggs came one way, scrambled. "Too much fuss about over easy, over hard, blah-de-blah. No way poached."

Larry was the cook — breakfast and lunch; dinner, too, if given notice. That afternoon, he charmed us; took a break from the table out front where a rotating posse of friends sat and talked under the overhang that must have sheltered the pumps in the earlier gas station incarnation. He volunteered to watch over our laundry if we wanted to go exploring.

Larry and Veronika, we surmised, were a couple — possibly she owned Pokey's as well as the motel. She sometimes waited tables and helped in the kitchen. But this was Larry's turf, and he took pride in how it looked and how the food tasted as we found out the next morning, but that's getting ahead of the story.

We did go exploring. The town of Grand Rivers lies at the north end of Land Between the Lakes National Recreation Area in Kentucky. It's situated on a peninsula between the reaches of Kentucky Lake and Lake Barkley, adjacent

Tennessee Valley Authority reservoirs which are the result of dams on the Tennessee and Cumberland Rivers, respectively. The extensive area between the lakes is a forested peninsula forty miles long. We were in northwestern Kentucky, across the Ohio River from Illinois.

The temperature had receded somewhat so we drove here and there, the trees and winding roads and hills and serious lakes right and left, a change from the flatlands of Kansas and Missouri. Back in Grand Rivers, we retrieved clean clothes, showered, and changed for dinner.

That evening we made one of our few bad choices. Feeling refreshed, Cherie and I ventured out into the warm, spring evening. The oppressive heat had dissipated even further but still there was no mistaking that Southern humidity. We strolled up the street and dined at a restaurant mentioned in a guidebook called "Patti's."

Aha, I thought. The unusual name could be a variation of Sylvester Pattie and his son James Ohio Pattie, early adventurers and explorers of the American West. I knew they were from Kentucky; I later learned they were born in Bracken County just up the Ohio River from where we sat. In 1824, Sylvester was one of the first Americans to venture into Baja California and what is now New Mexico where, tragically, he died a captive of a Native American tribe. A plaque in San Diego's Presidio Park commemorates Sylvester Pattie's interment there as the first American to be buried on California soil. Son James Ohio tells the story in his journals.

So I inquired of our hostess. "Never heard of him," she said, turning away to seat other guests. Same question of our server and same answer.

"Do you know how the restaurant got its name?"
"No."
"Is there possibly a plaque or museum that might have information."
"Don't think so. So what y'all want for dinner?"

64

"Well, I'll be having a hamburger PATT . . ."
which was as far as I got before Cherie dug her nails into my
pant leg.

"I'd like a glass of red wine, please," Cherie said. "What
kind do you have?"

"No wine or beer served here," was the cordial reply
from between shiny Dixie-white teeth and an automated prom
princess smile.

I scuffed my chair preparing to leave. Again, Cherie's
restraint. "Okay, let us think it over."

This was not a franchise eatery, but an elaborately
decorated and crowded restaurant. Full tables were chatting
happily and looking content. Did we look like the Northwest
Blue-Staters we were? We ordered a perfectly ordinary meal,
over-priced, and left.

No Pattie, no wine, no service — I mulled over making a
sign.

Later we asked Larry and Veronika. Both were polite and
didn't say "I told you so," but the inference was clear. It didn't
sound like small town competition, a Hatfield-McCoy kind of
thing. More likely, over-stated pretension versus down-home
comfort.

Next morning, Larry's breakfast was as advertised. He
roused himself from a beat-up sofa where he'd slept since
o-dark-thirty and fixed me scrambled eggs, crispy bacon, pan-
fried potatoes from somewhere in Heaven, and whole wheat
toast and scrumptious berry jam from an unlabeled pint jar.
Coffee made to order. I won't reveal what it cost. Just say it felt
like thievery.

We took our time before leaving. While Cherie went
back and packed (I'd already done mine), Larry and I sat at a
table out in front of the shop. Black wrought-iron mesh chairs
matched the table and we stretched out our legs onto the vacant
ones. He drank a beer and I had more coffee. I took my time,
but plied him with questions about the town and surrounds.

He'd moved south from Michigan after a marital split-up. The weather, the town, the scene, and I guessed Veronika suited him fine.

"Nice rig," he said nodding toward the car.

"Let's take a look."

He circled the car, at one point crouching down and inspecting the all-around disc brakes. I opened the hood and we both shook our heads at the bewildering, precisely engineered clutter of pumps, pipes, gauges, reservoirs, valve covers, belts, a shiny air cleaner, and somewhere in there an engine block and cylinder heads.

Larry said, "I remember back in the day when you'd open the hood ..."

I finished, " ...and you could see the ground."

He asked, "Uh, what do you think about me taking it just down the street and back."

"You'll have to ask the owner." I nodded toward our cabin.

He didn't push it. He asked if *we'd* like a spin, motioning to a spiffy boat on his trailer in the parking lot with a big Evinrude and a tiny electric fishing motor clamped to the stern. We politely declined, time constraints being what they were.

Larry lent me a hose to finish a bad carwash I'd paid for. We repacked the car. The commercial ice machine across the street was out of order, so Larry went back in the store and brought us some. Free. Larry's and Veronika's hospitality and place on the planet was to us what this excursion of ours was about. Appearances, and worse, preconceived notions of what *other* people are like in their own niches in this country are misleading.

We pulled out of the Grand Rivers Inn. Across the street at Pokey's was Veronika and her male "harem" — the same five or six fellas including Larry sitting once more around the table drinking coffee and talking and listening in the warm midday out of the sun. Round guys and thin, middle-aged and older, gray hair, one bald, overalls, levis and wide suspenders, flannel shirts, fisherman's vests — and Veronika in her skirt and blouse and orange sandals. We pulled over and said good-bye's.

I envied them. The easy camaraderie in a quiet town, none anxious to be anywhere else, or so it seemed, a pace of life that said "What's the hurry?" Maybe there'd been unemployment or a clobbering by a sub-prime sucker loan or a taking to the cleaners by an ex-spouse, a death. But whatever the stories, I let myself appreciate the grace as Larry topped off coffees and offered a slug of liquid out of a small brown bottle.

We beeped the horn and drove off. They waved back. We plan to return someday and eat a delicious, ridiculously low-priced meal before taking a spin on Kentucky Lake in Larry's boat. Maybe Veronika will come along.

# 10

# Blue Ridge Parkway

How embarrassing when a disturbing and quintessential male trait is brought to one's attention by one's spouse. It's worse when there's a third-party witness. The ever-patient Cherie found the event simply amusing.

It was a dark and rainy night. Driving to Asheville, North Carolina, all the way from Between the Lakes, we were later than we'd planned to be and low on gas. We pulled in at a nondescript Gas 'n Go and stopped next to the pumps. I got out and walked behind the car. Filling up our excellent vehicle, the Audi, first requires a light push on the flush-to-the-fender side door that conceals the gas cap, and the little door then springs open. Usually. I gave it a few taps. It didn't flip open. So I pushed harder on each corner but still nothing happened. It stayed closed like a stubborn three year-old's mouth facing a spoonful of cough medicine. The procedure had worked fine for three thousand miles. Why not now?

A motorist pulled in behind us, also driving an Audi, but a later model. The driver got out, I opened our trunk, and we took a look. His wife and two small children waited in their car. We found we could remove the felt-lined interior paneling on the right side of the trunk, but this wasn't going to help. The gas filler apparatus was too far forward and the way was blocked by a metal wall. There was no way to get where I needed to go.

If you're confused by now, imagine me. Did I mention it was raining? We were under a canopy but the wind was blowing and droplets flew hither and thither. The Good Samaritan and I looked at each other and shrugged. I was hungry and tired from a long day of driving across Tennessee.

Unnoticed, Cherie was standing behind us, and what was she doing? Reading the *owner's manual*, a 200-plus page booklet in small print I'd promised never to consult after scanning the bewildering table of contents.

She said, "Do you think …?"

What? Read the directions? Instead, like generations of my sex, the ones with the Y chromosome, I pushed harder on the indisputably solid metal interior wall and saw no way past the obstruction.

"Hey Honey," Cherie said. "There should be a plastic wire in there with a loop thingy on the end. It's supposed to be red. Take a look where you pulled off that inside paneling."

With an indulgent sigh, I shifted the flashlight to my left hand and leaned in. Whaddya know! A red plastic loop thingy! A quick pull and the renegade door flipped open. My new male friend and I didn't look at each other. I hoped his wife hadn't figured out what had happened. I mumbled a thank-you, he walked back to his car, and I filled up.

As I pulled away, my loving spouse of so many years replaced the owner's manual in its leatherette folder, snapped it shut, and didn't say a word. Later, she did confess that seeing me start around to the side of *her* car with a large screwdriver in my hand was what had sent her to the glove compartment. But seriously ….

The day had been a long one. For the first week of our travels, we'd floated with the current, hauling out as the mood struck us. Now, the 9th of May, we had to stick our paddles deeper into the water and stroke hard if we were to make it to niece, her hubby, and grandnieces in Fairfax, Virginia, by Mother's Day. It changed the dynamic from cruising to challenging, not the least because *three days* is the recommended time to traverse the Blue Ridge Parkway which we didn't want to miss.

Thus, with apologies to Tennessee Mountaineer fans, we

stuck to the Interstate. We took a pass on Nashville — Opryland, Dollywood, a replica of the Parthenon in "The Athens of the South" — and, with its eight hundred churches, the "Buckle of the Bible Belt". Nor did we stop and enjoy a riverboat cruise on the Star of Knoxville or visit the Women's Basketball Hall of Fame in that fine city. We did see the Great Smoky Mountains in the distance and their trademark blue haze as we crossed into North Carolina, but we couldn't afford the time to detour and explore.

Our destination was Asheville, North Carolina, where Zelda Fitzgerald spent her tragic last days and also the site of that Gilded Age icon, the Biltmore House. We stopped in Asheville also because it was Thomas Wolfe's hometown. His "fictional" memoir, Look Homeward Angel, written in a genre he pretty much invented, so thinly disguised its two-hundred-plus characters that Wolfe took off for Europe after it was published and stayed away for eight years.

Wolfe's family home is a National Landmark. Both Harvard and the University of North Carolina have archived his work. He is on a postage stamp. He died at 37. We didn't go see his birthplace, but being in a celebrated author's hometown resonated — think Kellogg, Idaho, or Hannibal, Missouri. In addition to Wolfe, a list of Southern writers goes on and on: Eudora Welty, John Grisham, Carson McCullers, Flannery O'Connor, Cormac McCarthy, Anne Tyler, Anne Rice, James Lee Burke, Katherine Anne Porter, James Dickey, Richard Ford, Truman Capote, Robert Penn Warren, James Faulkner, Tennessee Williams, and of course Harper Lee. "Southern Gothic" is too narrow a definition, but unusual characters and sinister events do seem to lurk in most of their work.

Following the gas station fiasco, we doubled down and had a terrible meal at a fast food joint and barely found the passable motel where we'd booked a room. The next day, rested and with spirits renewed, we enjoyed an outdoor breakfast on a warm morning in the heart of Asheville at the Tupelo Honey

Cafe. We strolled a bit and browsed quaint shops in the vintage downtown.

The Blue Ridge Parkway is a meandering 45-mph byway that runs from outside of Asheville and on into Virginia for 469 miles along the crest of the Blue Ridge Mountains. It is as beautiful and memorable a stretch of Americana as there is. Constructed as a Depression Era Civilian Conservation Corps project, parking areas along the way are bordered by signature knee-high CCC stone boundary walls and overlook the Shenandoah Valley of story and song and the Virginia piedmont that stretches eventually to the Atlantic. We took our time for seventy of those miles — early wildflowers, misty waterfalls, gorgeous views, and lots of turn-outs.

We stopped for lunch and took a short hike to a waterfall. What to do next? Dallying along at 45 miles per hour, striking scenery notwithstanding, wasn't going to work. The ground still to cover ahead of us was daunting, so with a wave and regrets we abandoned the Parkway in order to make better time. "Better time" is not what happened. For miles on end, we negotiated curves and two-lane straightaways on back road after back road in rural Virginia. It was lovely countryside, but darkness was approaching and traffic and towns were tedious.

When we finally got to Roanoke after dark, finding lodging was also a problem. It was graduation weekend. There are three colleges in the area: Roanoke University, Hollins College, and Virginia Polytechnic Institute. A half hour of phone calls yielded the last available room in a forgettable franchise hotel. Plus, we wouldn't have time to stop in nearby Blacksburg and visit Virginia Tech, Cherie's dad's college for which he wrote their *alma mater* back in the day.

The late, estimable Ernest Taylor Sparks, was a wonderful musician — a magnificent pianist, classical, pop, you name it. He learned the trade at the side of his father, and each of them at one time or another played speakeasies in Washington, D.C. My prospective father-in-law did present a challenge to me early on, however, when he learned that his adored daughter was about to marry a *lawyer* and one who hailed from *California*! Strikes one and two. All that was left would be for me to swing and miss a low and outside fastball he'd throw for the third strike. As it turned out, the only swinging that took place was on a golf course. We shared a love of the game, and love of a well-wrought martini. I was his new good buddy!

That Ernie Sparks could be a challenge, though, was clear. We were playing golf one day and, horror of horrors, someone in the group behind us teed off and sent a golf ball rolling past us. This is a cardinal *faux pas*. You don't applaud between symphony movements, you don't forget your wedding anniversary, and you don't hit into the group ahead of you on any golf course.

Without hesitating, new father-in-law Ernie approached the offending golf ball, took his stance, waggled his club, and fired the ball *back* at the interlopers still on the tee. Yours truly turned and headed for the green in a hurry, but there was no pursuit.

For whatever reason, graduations or karmic payback, we endured another late dinner and, too tired to complain, tumbled into bed.

All would be well. Fairfax and family lay ahead.

# 11

# Intermezzo

*Fairfax*

> The interest I take in my neighbor's nursery
> Would have to grow, to be even cursory ...
> > Ogden Nash (1902 — 1971)

Poor Ogden Nash. Luckily he didn't live to see Facebook and other Internet detritus and the daily, eager expressions of everything from Halloween costumes and toddlers' birthdays to teeners' prom dates and graduation hats and gowns. I won't even start about puppies, kittens, and hamsters.

Presciently, Nash continued with:

> And I would that performing sons
> and nephews
> > Were carted away with the daily refuse
> And I hold that frolicsome daughters
> and nieces
> > Are ample excuse for breaking leases.

Trivia buffs might be interested in knowing that a pre-Revolutionary ancestor of Ogden Nash founded Nashville, Tennessee.

Ignoring the poet's sardonic advice, this narrative will herewith take a break at the halfway point in our cross-country venture for a brief sketch of our time with relatives, big and small. I will begin with the grand-niece who would have turned even grumpy old Ogden's head.

Naomi Rockmann was then four, going on ten. She lives in Fairfax, Virginia, with her mom and dad and baby sister.

She adores her Aunt Cherie. She even warmed up to her Uncle Dick after he taught her the worthy skill of making s'mores. Little sister Blake, one and a half, is charming as well despite suffering from a nasty cold while we visited. Even runny-nosed kids are precious with a grin like hers.

We arrived in Fairfax the evening before Mother's Day. Tired after ten days of driving, we crashed in Kevin and Alison Rockmann's downstairs guest bedroom hoping to sleep in. Good luck with that. At 6:30 am, we heard one-and-a-half year-old running footsteps overhead. I buried my head under the pillow and tried to fall back asleep.

Cherie wasn't so lucky. She tossed and turned a bit until

she noticed tiny fingers reaching around the edge of our bedroom door, then a hand. Naomi's anxious little face peered in to see if Aunt Cherie was awake yet. Aunt Cherie, one eye opened, nodded. Naomi whispered "Is Uncle Dick awake?" Cherie lied, and hushed, "No, Sweetie, so we have to be quiet." Bless my wonderful wife.

Naomi's mother Alison is Cherie's niece. She teaches high school English. Her admirable goal is to convince at least a few students each year that texting isn't writing and literature didn't begin with *Twilight*. There is a golden throne reserved for her in Heaven.

Husband Kevin is a professor at George Mason University. His subject is communication in areas like effective advocacy and workplace negotiation. You know, people with differing opinions conversing constructively with one another. The irony of teaching the subject across the Potomac River from the Nation's Capitol is not lost on him.

That morning, Cherie bravely got up. Naomi was delighted. I weighed the pros and cons for a bit, bedcovers in disarray, then surrendered. Plus, I smelled breakfast. I fumbled into my clothes, threw cold water on my face, and guiltily stumbled upstairs into the morning melee of three adults and a four year-old in various stages of eating, feeding Blake in her highchair, clearing a place at the table for me, rinsing dishes, pouring coffee, passing around pancakes and eggs, listening to Naomi tell a story, Kevin trying to discuss the plan for the day, and Alison and Cherie catching up on the first installment of everything they had to catch up on.

I stopped eating and just watched. I got a lump in my throat. How *true* this all was. "True" is the word that came to mind; that, and how incredibly lucky we were, all six of us.

This was going to be fun. Early reveille be damned!

As the all-too-brief three days went on, we took long walks in glorious spring weather, swung and teeter-tottered in a park, admired gardens, kibitzed about neighbors, ate too much delicious food, played with dolls and toys, went out for pizza, talked and talked and talked, and made the aforesaid s'mores around a flagstone fire pit that polymath Kevin had built on their cozy patio.

Fairfax County takes great pride in its urban forest and well it should. The path we took to the children's park meandered through woods of red maple, American beech, tulip trees, oak, holly and hickory, white-blossomed dogwood, and various evergreens. On the way home, Naomi stopped at dandelions and we blew the fuzz into the air. Blake fell asleep in her stroller. Alison and Kevin's yard is surrounded by stately trees and was abloom with glorious azaleas — bright red, pink, and purple — and enormous rhododendrons. Their vegetable garden was popping up new shoots. A rope swing twenty feet high sailed back and forth with one of the kids in it.

Alison took a well-deserved personal day from teaching to spend quality time with Cherie. I went into D.C. to have lunch with a long-time friend and walk down familiar streets enjoying the sun, and yes, the heat.

Cherie was born in Washington (fourth generation!) and grew up in a Maryland suburb, but is outspoken about not wanting to spend more than the minimal time there because of the heat. On the other hand, I don't mind it — up to a point. I remember disembarking at Dulles Airport years ago to visit my parents and feeling the blast of Down East heat that slammed me the minute flight attendants opened the airline cabin door. At my folks' house, the upstairs guest bedroom looked out on their lush backyard and I'd keep the window open to listen to the birds and smell the air.

Not minding the heat "up to a point" means that putting on a suit and tie each day did become tiresome during the four separate times I lived and worked in Washington. The steam-heat in summer was challenging to this boy from the West Coast. The city was built on a swamp at the confluence of the Potomac and Anacostia Rivers on land that, understandably, neither Virginia or Maryland had any use for.

It was only in the high 80s the day I had lunch with my friend. We ate at the House of Representatives Longworth Building cafeteria surrounded by busy staffers and young interns clattering and nattering and solving the Nation's problems — or comparing micro-brews. After lunch, I took a leisurely stroll down Independence Avenue, along the Mall, crossed in front of the Capitol, and wandered up Constitution Avenue. Old haunts.

I get misty-eyed standing in front of the Capitol building. It's enormous, and blazes white in the sun. I am second to none in lamenting the current state of politics — I did capital "P" Politics for a living for most of my adult life — and today's version just plain hurts in my gut. But, for all the many, many faults of current (and plenty of former) participants, U.S. government remains a stirring symbol for me. People in fifty diverse states and in thousands of diverse cities and counties can go to polls on Tuesdays and vote.

I walked on, found a Starbucks, and people-watched for an hour before returning to the Metro station and zipping back to Fairfax in air-conditioned comfort.

### New York City

Time came to say goodbyes. We left Naomi in charge of the garden and stashed the car in the Rockmanns' driveway. The Amtrak Acela took us to New York City. The Acela from

Washington arrives at Penn Station. The ride north was a breeze — comfy seats, no pesky check-in, baggage a snap, a bar car with munchies — a safe, smooth high-speed ride to New York in under three hours and in a "quiet car." No cell phones or even loud talking.

A short cab ride later, we stashed our luggage at son Rick's flat in the Chelsea neighborhood and stashed ourselves at Le Grainne, a French restaurant we like around the corner at Ninth and Twenty-first Street.

We sat outside in the sun, drank dark coffee, ate *pain au chocolat*, and reminisced about our time in Paris. Past us went the endless parade of yellow NYC cabs racing, dog-walkers leashing, joggers jogging, tourists yakking, twenty-somethings earbudding, and the polyphony of purposeful New Yorkers heading to work. Who are all these people! New York never stops bustling, all eight and a half million people, day and night. It's possible to walk a block and never hear a word of English. Running shorts, outlandish cycling unitards, keffiyehs, chadors, short skirts, long skirts, t-shirts, no-shirts, here and there a sport coat and tie. Wing-tips, loafers, sandals, running shoes, no-shoes.

Chelsea's streets are tree-lined, and Rick has a small backyard. He'd walk a few blocks to work where he was a big shot at The High Line. His brother Michael lives across Manhattan on the Lower East Side where he runs the coffee shop he owns, called Lost Weekend NYC. Both of them love the day-in/day-out hustle, crowds, subways, non-stop lives they live — even the noise. Rick has a humidifier that he runs as white noise even when it's not needed because he says it gets too quiet at night sometimes (!).

Highlights of the visit:

~ a guided tour of the (now opened) third and final phase of The High Line; millions of visitors a year stroll along its three-mile elevated walkway, for free;

~ hanging out at Lost Weekend having coffee with a wonderful friend I worked with in Olympia; she's the staff director for the New York legislature's first and only Korean-American member;

~ a visit with adorable brand-new grand-nephew Everett and his parents in the up-and-coming Gowanus section of Brooklyn; we watched as Mexican dinner was ordered via a smart phone's "Seamless" app because no one calls in a delivery order any more;

~ a seriously confusing subway ride to get to Brooklyn and interesting route back across the Manhattan Bridge and into the city; the savvy, female Ecuadorian hired-car driver argued with Rick about the fastest way to *his* apartment;

~ the purchase of over-the-top bright yellow Nikes at the New York HQ; and,

~ my usual visit to the Metropolitan Museum of Art.

The members' dining room at the Met (I belong, of course) was typically crowded. I hadn't made a reservation but my hostess M'bida recognized me with a smile and escorted me to a table by the window. She looked smashing, as usual — small diamond posts instead of gold hoops, eyelashes to die for, legs of an Olympic sprinter. I ordered my usual, *plancha* black sea bass with roasted Brussels sprouts and hazelnuts.

Jay-Z came in and heads turned. Beyoncé was not with him. Solange was. The clatter of silverware and wine glasses resumed quickly. After all, this was New York and celebrities are as common as the pigeons. Diners were more concerned about the downpour outside. Thunderstorms had threatened all day, and the wind flipped spring-green branches back and forth just beyond the cantilevered window where I sat overlooking Central Park. No one even noticed my shoes.

Actually, none of this happened. I made it up. All but the lunch part and the weather.

I'd gone to the Met especially to see the Goya-Altamira Family exhibit. I was unmoved. Certainly Señor Goya deserves his place among the Great Masters. (Who am I to say!) But how many portraits of Spanish nobility are too many? He did have fortunate connections along the way and they all wanted to be painted, but so many of the faces (not only the principals, but others in the paintings) had the same pre-Renaissance, mannequin-like look to them. Contrast, for instance, the troop of soldiers looking on in the "Surrender at Breda" by Velasquez. Maybe I'd been spoiled by visiting the Prado two years previously.

I moved on. The crowds inside the Met and outside on the fabled steps were crazy, raincoats and umbrellas, and confusion. The cab ride back downtown was the usual Formula One speedway. Construction was everywhere.

I'm not unused to New York and the people there, but for some reason this stopover tired us out. We had a very special dinner with our kids that evening and bade our usual tearful goodbyes.

Cherie flew home from Newark on the 17th to attend to a Domestic ObliGation we had. There was no emergency — we'd planned the trip that way for ease of mind, four-legged and two.

My challenge of driving west for three-thousand miles solo was an unknown.

# 12

# Interstates, Near Escapes and Fly-over States

Saturday morning May 17th the return crossing began pretty much as expected. I took the Acela back to Washington D.C. — by myself — and picked up our car at Kevin and Alison's house. After good-bye hugs from our lovely hosts in Fairfax, I rejoined US 50, but only for a quick five miles to the Washington Beltway (I-495).

Around I went, clockwise, crossed the Potomac, then exited onto I-270 north until a stop in Hagerstown, Maryland, poised just south of Messrs. Mason's and Dixon's survey line. For those taking notes, the Mason-Dixon Line originally had nothing to do with the Civil War and its subsequent politics. It resolved an Eighteenth Century border dispute between the colonies of Pennsylvania and Maryland. Hagerstown is notable, however, for being equidistant between Gettysburg and Antietam (or Sharpsburg, if you're still a Reb) and the town was a crossroads of many back and forth campaigns during the Civil War.

After lunch at a Tim Horton's (eh!) and back in the car, the digital compass display in the rearview mirror said "NW." Unlike the first half of the trip, I wanted to make better time, mostly on Interstates but not without stops along the way.

Interstate 270 winds through the pretty hills of northern Maryland — they call them "mountains" — and intersects the Pennsylvania Turnpike whereupon the mirror compass switched to "W." The Turnpike has been around since the 1790s, and what a success! People who use the road pay for it as they go.

Ohio, Indiana, and Illinois got the message and later followed suit. No free ride, as it were, until Wisconsin. A saving grace: Many of the service plazas — facilities for gas, restrooms, *et al*, that don't require exiting from the turnpike — have Starbucks.

Thus far, the drive was pleasant enough, and I know there's important history along the way, but I was on a mission to get past Chicago by the end of the next day. It's also a fact that eastern highways are usually surrounded by trees — lots and lots of bushy, green trees, abundant in spring foliage and allowing only intermittent views of the countryside. At several clearings that day, the view included billboards promoting coal, to wit: "The sun doesn't always shine. The wind doesn't always blow. What will you do then? Think COAL!"

I stopped at Youngstown, Ohio, had dinner, and got a good night's rest. This turned out to be a very good idea because the next morning, the trouble started. After the calm Interstate through the land of Buckeyes and Hoosiers where Interstate 90 parallels the shore of Lake Erie came the storm. *Chicago!*

Serious advice: Stop! Do not pass Go. Turn around. Find another route. Do not under any circumstance attempt the highways around Chicago unless you give the city wide berth — I mean seriously wide, like a couple of states' worth. Note, I wasn't trying to drive *through* it, just negotiate the outskirts.

Circumnavigating the Windy City (on a Sunday morning no less) was like following a strand of noodle through a huge bowl of top ramen, at top speed.

Before I knew it I was going 75 — posted 55! — hovering in the right lane behind an eighteen wheeler with some jerk on my tail. In each of the four lanes to my left cars passed me like I was standing still. ("Eighty-five is the new fifty-five," later said my nephew, a native, over the phone and laughing.)

The drivers were twisted, egomaniacal assholes, clutching the wheel like pissed off kids in bumper cars and dodging and weaving. Why were they all so angry? On and on we raced, hubcap to hubcap and bumper to bumper, the lead car changing from time to time, tailgating, swerving to avoid even crazier motorcyclists. The term "death wish" crossed my mind.

Understand this: I'm not timid nor inexperienced in big city wacko traffic; viz, Washington D.C., LA, SF Bay Area; one harrowing time down I-25 between Boulder and Denver set the bar pretty high, or should I say low.

This day, I challenged The Reaper twice myself, making life-threatening course changes through the diagonally striped no-man's land beyond the marked exit off-ramp simply to stay on the main highway. I think I sailed past a toll booth without paying.

Construction and "exit temporarily closed" signs were surprise wildcards. Off-ramps, on-ramps, toll booths, lanes closed, semis, dump trucks, and not a cop in sight. And that's not the worst of it. How was I going to get where I was supposed to go? Where was my trusty co-driver with the map? Back home sleeping off jetlag on a Sunday morning in our comfy bed two time zones away, that's where.

I squinted ahead as far as I could see, between glances in side-mirrors and the rearview. Directional signs loomed up out of nowhere, too late to make the correct exit. Wouldn't it make logical sense that I-294 should split off of I-94? Nope, it takes off of *I-90* further on, past the I-94 off-ramp. I-294 actually goes north, south, and east and west, *simultaneously*. I would have thought that a cartological impossibility.

When finally the "continue on 294" sign popped up, it was an impossible one hundred yards ahead and I flew past it. I took the next exit and wandered around on side streets and busy arterials for an hour trying to get back where I wanted to be. Through sheer luck and Divine intervention, I regained I-90 and drove endless miles to Rockford, Illinois, then north into Wisconsin.

Crossing to safety, I pulled over, turned off the car next to a field of curious cows, and had a good cry. Thanks to a drive-through coffee stand, an iced *decaf* mocha and a chocolate chip cookie soothed my nerves. Back on the road, I cruised along without incident along with lots of other, sane, Badger Staters.

The town of Tomah, Wisconsin (pop. 9,000) is where the two northernmost, cross-country Interstates, I-90 and I-94, split and don't reconnect until far-off Billings, Montana. I checked in at a motel, tossed and turned, but finally got to sleep. Next morning under a cloudy sky, I drove into town to find breakfast. Seeing nothing that caught my eye on the first pass, I made inquiries and was directed to a nondescript eatery with, significantly, several cars parked in front.

"Nondescript" is a generous term, but after years of practice I've learned not to judge a small town restaurant by its decor — in this case "un-decor." The sign outside looked like it was hand-drawn on chalk board, smudged but readable. Inside was familiar chrome-and-vinyl seating and nothing on the walls unless you count three framed and faded color photographs of successive softball teams and a poster advertising Aspen. "We Don't Care" is the term I've invented for the ambience of such a place, and I mean that as a compliment. It was clean, friendly, and good enough for the dozen Kiwanians yukking it up down the way. The Standard — bacon and eggs, hash browns, whole wheat toast, and good coffee — came to $11.95.

A nice start in a nice town. After the dizzying drama the day before, it was beyond nice. "Normal" is a better word.

Looking down 35,000 feet from a Boeing 737, state boundaries are not well-marked. They aren't marked at all! Since most airline pilots are home-based in large population centers, east and west, they've usually switched on the automatic pilot and dozed off well before their westbound jet crosses Lake Michigan. Somewhere down there Wisconsin becomes Minnesota, Minnesota turns into South Dakota, and so on. "Fly-over states" is the snide term.

I eschew such haughty disdain! Of course I had little choice did I, two thousand miles from home in a gravity-bound vehicle, top velocity (courtesy of liberal speed limits) of 80 mph? Press on, I did, and I'd do it again in a minute. Well, *lots* of minutes.

I pushed on after breakfast in Tomah and in less than an hour crossed the Mississippi River at La Crosse (of course). This was not nearly the picturesque event as on the way east, crossing the river by ferry from Missouri to Kentucky. This day, the heavens had opened and it was pouring. The busy, four-lane bridge high over the river was under construction to repair deteriorating decking. Good choice, I thought, since the wind-blown, churning grey water of the Mississippi was a long way down. The rain continued off and on through most of Wisconsin.

When I crossed into Minnesota, the sun came out. I slowed down, took an exit, and moseyed along a scenic byway that followed the Root River. As so often happened, this was a worthy detour.

Take Lanesboro, Minnesota, for example. The seven hundred and fifty-four folks who call Lanesboro their home live in a gem of a town, proving again a refreshing theory that I continued to take note of, a refrain in a now-familiar tune. Nearly all towns have their own sense of identity, their own traditions no matter how small or unobtrusive at first glance.

A blip on the map along a road in southern Colorado has a

central park. Scoot over a block from the main street of Resume Speed, Kansas, and find a city hall and a museum surrounded by grass and trees. Always look for the signature brown sign with white lettering that points the way to the birthplace of a favorite son or daughter — writer, senator, explorer. Another sign tells of the Rhubarb Festival coming up the first week of June. Be sure to wave at the old guys sitting in front of the drugstore watching unfamiliar cars go by.

History is ubiquitous. So is sense of place. Civic pride, however muted, will be discovered by the observant.

Speaking of observant, so it was that I was lazily driving into Lanesboro, Minnesota, idly watching the pretty scenery, when I rounded a corner, slammed on the brakes, skidded to a stop, and avoided taking out … a turkey!

The iconic feathered critter was smack in the middle of the road, very large and uncaring. There he stood — I was on *his* turf — thoughtfully appraising his chances against the ton of motor vehicle idling in front of him. He didn't give an inch. It was a stand-off. I turned off the engine.

Time passed. He won. With a flutter and not a fare-thee-well, he acknowledged his victory and waddled off. I drove on — but not, I confess, without thinking of cranberry sauce, creamed onions, mashed potatoes and gravy, and stuffing.

Around the next bend was a city limit sign announcing the "Hub of the Root River Trail System," Lanesboro, which is also the official Rhubarb Capital of Minnesota. Besides which, Lanesboro serves as a mecca for, what else, wild turkey hunting. I asked myself, how does one shoot a turkey? I don't mean the moral question, though that bothers me. I mean, does one use a shotgun or a rifle? And what part to aim for? The feathery body armor looks equal to the task of deflecting pellets, and why mutilate that magnificent gobbler wattle by firing at its head? I decided not to ask.

Beyond Lanesboro, the Root River meanders along for thirty miles through lush hardwood forests, passes sandstone cliffs, and is well-known to canoeists, hikers, cyclists, and birders. A bald eagle soared by. The next town was Houston. (Austin lay several miles ahead.) I stopped and stretched my legs. Lo and behold, across the street was a coffee spot called, naturally, "Barista."

The small establishment sat on a corner where the town's two main streets, the only ones with stop signs, intersected. Next to the shop and past a deck for outside seating were rusty railroad tracks and a weathered green and black boxcar with faded white lettering on the side, relic of the defunct, short-line Minnesota, Dakota, and Western Railway.

The proprietors, an enthusiastic young couple, had visited San Francisco once, briefly. That was the extent of their research into the national coffee fad that they'd guessed right about and made happen in an isolated corner of Minnesota far south of the metropolis of Minneapolis. Photographs and paintings they'd hung on the walls looked professionally done. Next to a distressed oak counter with a real cash register hung a poster announcing a performance of "Our Town" at the theater down the street. "Tickets here," it said. Listening to the hiss of steam and basking in the welcome aroma of espresso made me homesick. I still had a long way to go.

After a latté fix, I drove through nearby Preston (the Trout Capital of Minnesota) and eventually wound my way back to Interstate 90. I did have miles to go, on a stretch of road straight as a die, and I passed towns like Albert Lea and Blue Earth (home of *both* the Eskimo Pie and the Jolly Green Giant). I didn't stop until Sioux Falls where I spent the night; five hours of driving, 370 miles, and not an Illinois license plate in sight.

# 13

# The Badlands

What a river, the Missouri!

I stopped and lunched May 20th, in Chamberlain, South Dakota, beside the Big River. For an uninterrupted hour in a pretty park with tables and benches and canopies and clean fire pits on a warm summer day midway across America, I cleansed my soul of the previous days' hard driving. I munched my signature road lunch: Triscuits topped with chunks of cheddar cheese, French's mustard, bread and butter pickles, and a Coke. Talk about cuisine! It was noon straight up.

With headwaters far to the west near the town of Three Forks, Montana, where the Jefferson, the Madison, and the Gallatin Rivers flow together, the "Wide Missorah" bisects South Dakota, north to south, before jogging eastward to form the boundary with Nebraska. Remarkable, from where I sat, how much farther downstream the mighty river had yet to go before reaching St. Louis and the Mississippi. The Missouri's total length is over 2,300 miles.

Zipping along in a car in the 21st Century demands stopping and contemplating this, and trying to capture in one's mind in **bold** the magic and magnificence of Lewis and Clark's accomplishment. Here in the middle of South Dakota, they'd scarcely begun.

Earlier that morning, the city of Sioux Falls surprised me by how large it is. Over 150,000 people live there, nearly a third of South Dakota's population. Situated well southwest of Minneapolis, four hours northwest of Des Moines, and a long way from Rapid City on South Dakota's western boundary, the result is a cultural and commercial center for a large swath of northern Plains States territory. I strolled through the picturesque downtown streets that featured sculpture and novel renovation.

The namesake Falls of the Big Sioux River is surrounded by a spacious park with walkways, bike paths, a visitor center, and overlooks. I'd have lingered longer but I had plenty of territory to cover if I was going to make it to Rapid City. I planned to spend two days there seeing the Badlands, the Black Hills, and Mount Rushmore.

After lunch on the Missouri, my mind sailed away in one direction then off in another as one's does. I talked to myself. Not a big problem, I decided, as long as I didn't get into an actual conversation and start answering myself. There's a lot of open road in South Dakota, meaning not a lot of challenge in operating a vehicle, particularly in my vehicle which is a far better driver than I.

This is a good place to confess, I must add, to how different this solo half of the cross-country trek felt. Cherie's and my drive east had been one of exploration — pioneering, in a sense, of new places, new mores, new history, *sans* covered wagon. We had an agenda of sorts, but each town felt new, each bend in the road an unknown. Now, the goal was home and the roads were freeways, straight highways covering miles each day.

I missed my driving companion, of course, and not just for logistical reasons. Nor will I wax romantic … much. But we shared the excitement each new day brought. I think John Keats got it right when he wrote of Solitude, away from the jumbled heap of murky buildings and 'mongst boughs pavilion'd, he concluded:

> …it sure must be
> Almost the highest bliss of human-kind
> When to thy haunts *two* kindred spirits flee.
>                     (Emphasis mine)

So now, on my own, and even though I was experiencing places new to me, this return leg was a different journey. Solitude, which is often restorative (not loneliness; I wasn't sad), made hours pass into hours of mindless thought.

At one point as I daydreamed, however, I roused myself. I thought I sensed something in the air. Not a scent really, but a difference that felt, well, "atmospheric." The car windows were down and I put my hand and arm out, splaying my fingers as I often do, feeling the wind. Nothing actually smelled different, but looking ahead and in the rearview mirror and to the left and right across wide-open expanses of empty prairie, it dawned on me what it was.

I was back in the West.

Now, I enjoy the East Coast very much. As for "the West," my guess is that Plains Staters would likely dispute my lumping them in with latté drinking, fleece-wearing, Blue State Microsofties, or God-forbid Californians. But there was no mistaking it — the uninterrupted vistas, the expanses to the horizons, the Rockies ahead and the Pacific Coast where I've spent ninety percent of my life. I was heading home. My chest swelled. I took deep breaths. I felt palpable excitement. Pedal met metal.

I mean no offense either when I note that there aren't many photographically beautiful scenes in the middle of South Dakota. What there are are billboards, a redeeming feature actually what with little else eye-catching to look at. Billboards make interesting reading material and those in South Dakota along Interstate 90 had a uniqueness of their own.

Thankfully, they weren't jam-packed on top of one another like the approach to Dodge City. But take for instance three identical signs miles apart advertising "Dick's – 24 hour Toe Service." [sic]. Another sign said "Throttle Mania Wrestling" Maybe it said "Full Throttle Wrestling" — I can't be sure.

A prize for outdoor advertising should be awarded to a pair of billboards outside of Mitchell, South Dakota — *non*

*sequiturs*, one might say. One proudly boosted the "Corn Palace."
Attached to it — it was a double billboard — and just as large,
and also "not to be missed," was one that advertised the George
McGovern Museum.

Apparently, it was not enough that the proud son of South
Dakota suffered the second largest landslide presidential defeat
in American history, winning only Massachusetts and the
District of Columbia (seventeen lousy electoral votes) and lost to
Tricky Dick Nixon in the bargain. Today and every day, George
McGovern shares idle space in the minds of Dakotan passersby
with a monument to *maize*!

This South Dakota roadside sign doesn't take the
sweepstakes, however. That honor goes to an ad outside of
Pueblo, Colorado, pointing to a single-wide trailer on a dirty,
otherwise empty lot: "Non-Traditional Medical Treatment —
Special — $200 an ounce."

A billboard bonanza was yet to come, those advertising the
world-famous, nonpareil Wall Drug. Blazoned across sign after
sign on the Interstate for miles, huge billboards announce: "Free
ice water!" "Coffee — 5 cents." "Wait, there's more!"

Wall Drug is one of the uniquely American species that
includes Little America in Wyoming, Rock City in Georgia,
Mystery Spot near Santa Cruz, South of the Border, South
Carolina, and The Nut Tree — "California's Legendary Road

Stop." For this sort of *über* roadside attraction, the actual destination is no less interesting than the signage leading to it. Wall Drug reportedly spends $400,000 a year for hundreds of billboards between Minnesota and Billings, Montana. I exited the interstate and stopped. How could I not?

The place itself is an enclosed mini-metropolis, acres in size. It's a rabbit warren of room after room after over-stocked room. Hallways lead to other hallways and more rooms (somewhere there was a restaurant back in there) filled with every imaginable array of touristy glitz and glop and trinkets and trash. I wandered, mouth agape, and worried that I hadn't dropped bread crumbs to find my way back out.

Books and bobble-heads, candy and ballcaps, rocks and bronze statuettes, stuffed jackalopes, Christmas cards, postcards and posters, knives, refrigerator magnets and more. A vial of Annie Oakley Perfume caught my eye. So did a Founding Fathers Shotglass. I broke down and bought a monogrammed coffee mug.

After an hour, overdosed on geegaws, I stumbled back to the car. The free water *had* been refreshing, and okay, I love the coffee mug.

Of Wall Drug, Bill Bryson said, "It's an awful place, one of the world's worst tourist traps, but I loved it and I won't have a word said against it."

I forgot to mention the dinosaur. Eighty feet long with light bulbs for eyes?

After Wall Drug's version of reality, another type of surreal experience awaited this traveler farther along the way to Rapid City — one that rekindled a favorite memory. As a youngster, I listened to *The Lone Ranger* faithfully on the radio at night. (I *am* that old.) Readers younger than I will remember Clayton Moore and Jay Silverheels on the TV series. Zane Grey's iconic stories were riveting: the masked man, the silver bullets, "Hi-yo, Silver, away!," and the unforgettable William Tell Overture. In today's political correctness, we cringe at "Kemo Sabe," "Gettem-up, Scout," and the subservient, but always insightful Tonto, a "red man," as well we should. History always needs correcting.

That said, ahead lay the Badlands and I couldn't help wanting to . . .

> "Return with us now to those thrilling days of yesteryear, when from out of the past come the thundering hoofbeats of the great horse Silver! The Lone Ranger rides again!"

Often, my duo of heroes would be headed for the alluringly named wilderness. The bad guys the Lone Ranger and Tonto chased would be racing to the Badlands to escape into the maze. I needed to see for myself. I was not disappointed.

The wide-open expanse of South Dakota changes dramatically. The signature terrain lives up to its name — a unique and strange geological formation of buttes and pinnacles and spires, narrow spaces, sheer cliffs, and drop-offs. I set off on a trail from the parking area and lost my sense of direction after a handful of steps. Moving among the ridges and sentinels particularly on horseback would be impressive.

Interestingly, over half of the Badlands isn't that "bad." Native Americans used the mixed grass prairie flatlands as hunting grounds and the rivers for fishing for thousands of years. After Custer's defeat in 1876, tribal ghost dancers prayed that the white man would vanish and their hunting grounds would be restored. Today, in the Badlands, fifty or so miles north of the 1890 Wounded Knee Massacre, park operation duties and revenue is shared with the Oglala Sioux. The very least we could do, I thought.

Wall Drug and then the Badlands. As my oenological friends might say, "Now there's a pairing!" I did wonder if there might be a reason for the collection of oddities I found in the grass prairies of the Northern Plains. Was it the altitude (probably not) or perhaps the unrelenting open space; a place for something out of the ordinary along a largely empty stretch of highway where the sky disappears into nothingness far ahead?

Whatever the cause, it turned out that the Corn Palace, Wall Drug, and the Badlands were only the most recent, and would not be the last, digressions into a parallel reality.

I drove on to Rapid City. Eight and a half hours after the morning in Sioux Falls. All in *one* western state.

# 14

# Close Encounters

Mount Rushmore

I was looking forward to Mt. Rushmore. Kitsch, possibly, but impressive kitsch, I hoped. Sadly, I ran into two glitches. ("Kitsch glitches"?)

Mt. Rushmore is a mountain over a mile high, well above 3,750-foot Rapid City, and it was socked in. High clouds in Rapid City led to mist, then rain, the higher I drove.

That mightn't have been too bad; I was willing to wait awhile to see if the weather improved. Up the winding mountain road I drove, and turned onto the only access road to the parking area. I was stopped by a toll booth. A nice young lady leaned out and wanted $11 as a "concessionaire fee." Huh? In a National Park? I pulled out my trusty National Park Lifetime Senior Pass. Nope, not accepted.

> Me: "Is there another way to see the monument if I
> don't want to visit the "concession"? (I made the double
> two-finger quotation marks.)

Toll booth person: "No."

Me: "It's clouded in."

Her: "They say it might clear up."

Me: "And it might not, meaning I've paid for nothing."

Her: "I'm sorry, sir."

Me: "How come a concession gets to charge a fee to get into a National Park? Concessions, in my experience, pay the *park* a fee to operate on government property."

Her: "I don't know."

Me: "Okay, I'll skip it today. Show me where to turn around." There was now a line of cars behind me.

Her: "There isn't one."

Me: "Can I drive past you and just turn around?"

Her: "No."

Me: "Are you willing to go to the cars behind me and tell them to let me back up?"

Her: "I can't leave the booth."

Me: "Does it strike you that this is extortion? False imprisonment, possibly?"

Not willing to lawyer up, I paid the lousy $11. It turns out that Mt. Rushmore is a "national memorial" run by something called the Mt. Rushmore Society. So much for the Land of the *Free*.

Ticked off, I drove straight through the parking lot and out the other side. With a superior grin, I looked at all the cars from other states, their occupants trudging through the mist and into a modern building that I'm sure was loaded with information and nice pictures, in search of a sculptured mountain they probably wouldn't be able to see for real.

Speaking of which, as far as I could tell, there was no other way to see the famous granite-faced chief executives, so I never did. I have no basis upon which to decide between Disneyfication and serious importance. Parallel realities? In either case, I did miss seeing Cary and Eva Marie rappelling off Abe Lincoln's nose. I'll get the video on Netflix. And the scene on the train ....

There still were the Black Hills, notable in their own right. I wound down the other side of the mountain and through the forest and rock formations that surround it. What I could see through the mist and low clouds was beautiful. I'd like to return some day and camp.

The small towns surrounding the National Memorial are, like Rapid City, understandably capturing every drop of tourist dollar they can. Who can blame them? Times are tough for cities.  I cruised through Keystone, for instance, which consisted of, end to end on both sides of the street, faux Western saloons, gift shops, gas stations, motels, realtors, an old-time bank, ice cream stands and laundromats. The only thing missing was a Starbucks which, come to think of it, might not have been allowed in. I had lunch at a friendly cafe in Custer City, then found a loop road the map said would take me through Custer State Park, also on my list. Guess what? A fee for entry, even just passing through. I was getting the picture.

Around I turned and backtracked, for free, to Rapid City.

Downtown Rapid City (pop. 76,000) is pleasant, despite the relentless flogging of Mt. PayMore: Mt. Rushmore Blvd, Mt. Rushmore Rest Stop, Mt. Rushmore Lawn Mower Repair, right on through town. Why hadn't they gone ahead and renamed the town? After all, Rapid Creek itself is only a smallish river that flows out of the Black Hills. They did rename the state. South Dakota used to be "The Sunshine State"; in 1980 it was changed to, you guessed it, "The Mt. Rushmore State."

Rapid City delights in US presidents — all of them. On corners and mid-block are statues in bronze or stone: John Adams looking all Adams-y — bald, vest, tails — like on a postage stamp; at another intersection, George Herbert Walker Bush poses in a suit and tie, one hand on a globe. I passed TR, dressed ready to charge up San Juan Hill, then smiling Harry Truman. At the next corner, I did a double-take wondering why Will Rogers was included. My mistake. It was Ronald Reagan in cowboy regalia, open-collared shirt, Stetson on his head, one foot on a rock, a hand on his knee. Farther on a sign announced that Barack Obama "is coming soon."

Also downtown is the historic Alex Johnson Hotel, carefully restored to original Nineteenth Century decor. Spend the night there only if you dare, I was informed. It's haunted. Seriously haunted, according to reported sounds of moans and tapping and creaking and apparitions slipping over transoms and into rooms. I went no farther than the lobby which was quaint and authentically furnished, but a little scary itself.

(A note regarding lodging in general. I must say I appreciate the newly advertised hierarchy of hospitality throughout the states. In descending order there are Comfort Inn Suites, Comfort Inn *and* Suites, Comfort Inns *ordinaire*; Best Western Premier, Best Western Plus, plain old BW; Holiday Inn Express, Holiday Inn; the ranked La Quintas, et cetera. You get the idea. Takes some of the guesswork out. Helps make choosing a motel easier, and easier on the pocketbook.)

My day in Rapid City ended well, topped off by an excellent dinner at an Italian restaurant next door to the Alex Johnson Hotel — not frightening at all unless you count the check. After settling up, I went back to my motel, peeked under the bed just to be safe, and slept undisturbed.

On to Wyoming … and this happened.

They asked me if I'd like to go back with them on their ship to their home world and live with their people. I declined. Said I had to get home, mow the lawn, keep a dental appointment, feed the cat, and pick up dry-cleaning.

"Nanuwingorobinki," their leader replied looking up at me, big-eyed and disappointed.

Then how about taking a short ride in their machine? he asked. I said sure, why not and we went aboard. The long ramp closed into its hatch with a hydraulic pfffft. I buckled in and in a flash, Devil's Tower was a tiny speck in the rearview monitor. In no time we were whipping around Alpha Centauri. Out the window, I saw that it *is* a triple star like the books say. It looks like one star to the naked eye, but in fact it is three: Alpha Centauri A and B, plus Proxima Centauri which, at 4.5 light-years, is the closest star to our solar system. Proxima is nearer than the other two by a tenth of a light-year — six hundred million miles, practically spitting distance.

Fast! You wanna talk fast? We made it to the Centauri system in twenty minutes. How much faster than the speed of light is that? My head ached trying to do the math.

The pilot motioned toward the Milky Way, but I shook my head. They didn't argue. The headman had left his wife back on my planet to do some shopping at Macy's and she had the checkbook *and* the credit card. Discover, of course.

We returned to an abandoned airstrip behind Devil's Tower that is not on any guide map or Google Maps but which I knew about. I won't say where it is; the NSA might find out. Back in the car, I waved out the window and drove off to find the National Monument grounds proper.

Devil's Tower is a few miles off Interstate 90 which cuts the northeast corner of Wyoming before going into Montana. On the way there is a turn-off to Ucross, Wyoming, famous to Cherie and me as the hometown of Craig Johnson, he of the Sheriff Longmire books (*The Cold Dish* and others). Some of the stories have been loosely translated for a series on A&E.

That humans have been fascinated by Devil's Tower, even before *Close Encounters of the Third Kind*, is obvious. How could it not be so? It's an 867-foot vertically striated monolith, visible for miles, erupting out of a picturesque valley hundreds of feet below its base. The domed area at the summit is an acre and a half in size. Devil's Tower is fifty million years old, and legends about it can be traced into prehistory for thousands of years. "There are things in nature that engender an awful quiet in the heart of man; Devil's Tower is one of them," according to one writer. (N. Scott Momaday, Pulitzer winning Native American poet.)

The closest I came to a non-fictional transcendent moment happened as I circumnavigated the base of the peak. A four-mile asphalt trail begins at the parking area and visitor center. Before long, it winds around and up and over granite boulders, some as large as a delivery truck. About halfway, I stopped to catch my breath. At the 4,000-foot elevation, in the noonday sun, a drink of water was imperative. A small group stood looking up at the mountain, gaping and photographing. Tiny creatures, two climbers, were making an ascent, as do over 5,000 people per year. They seemed to inch along and there was a lot of elevation to cover.

*Here's the naked-eye look.*

*Here's a close-up.*

I added extreme rock climbing to skydiving and
spelunking on the list of things I will depart this earth never
having attempted.

On my way out of the park, I pulled over beside a well-
populated prairie dog town. The cute little critters chased and
tumbled and dove down burrows, auditioning for a gig on
the Discovery Channel. I lingered there by the Belle Fourche
River, snacked on a granola bar, and admired 360º of limitless
gorgeous scenery.

It was time to resume the Interstate trail, as it had to be. I was hungry and ready for a close encounter with lunch. In Moorcroft, Wyoming, there was yet another unpretentious spot to eat called "Donna's." The parking lot in front full of pickup trucks and cars meant, as usual, that this would be a good choice.

As remarked upon in earlier episodes, what is unique about so many places like Donna's is their "un-uniqueness." There is no attempt to be cute or timely or *au courant* — plain tables and chairs, kitchen in plain view, plain-looking waitpersons, a couple of calendars on an empty wall next to an 8x10 black-and-white of three folks, arms around each other's shoulders, shotgun propped against a hip; a cash register that rings when you push the levers on the front. I had a great BLT, and fries that had been cooked right then, and a Coke.

At the next table was a pair of good old boys in cowboy hats; next to them, three elderly ladies (one *smoking!*); and down the way, a cute teenager sitting with her boyfriend and probably a dad and an uncle. In walked two Brits, of all people. They clunked motorcycle helmets on a table next to a window where they could keep an eye on their fully loaded Honda Gold Wings parked outside — one metallic blue, the other glossy black. They made themselves right at home and ordered tea. Of course. The waitress didn't blink and found a variety which seemed to suit.

I stopped and chatted them up on my way out. I ogled their machines out the window and they filled me in: XM radio, surround-sound, and iPod connectivity; heated handle grips and seat; and, to hear them talk, enough cc's to power a small plane. They'd drawn the line at customized fender ornaments — too "American," they politely said.

They'd flown to Chicago from London and picked up the bikes right off the line at the Marysville, Ohio, plant. I enjoyed the lingo: "chaps" weren't the leather garments they wore, rather the blokes they'd run into along the way; a "flat" wasn't an unfortunate mishap on the road, rather the place they'd rented in Seattle; a "fortnight" was how long they'd been on the road, not a campout in a Western military outpost.

The lass brought them sausage, fried potatoes, and eggs — as close as they'd get to bangers and mash — and they didn't complain. When one of them excused himself to use the loo, I bade them "cheerio" and toddled off.

Back on the road to the West, the Great State of Montana, and home.

# 15

# Montana ... and Home!

The Big Sky Country has fascinated me since childhood, dating from the time my dad handed me a copy of *The Way West* for which A.B. Guthrie won a Pulitzer Prize in 1950. Next I read Guthrie's earlier book, *The Big Sky,* and followed that with Irving Stone's *Men to Match My Mountains.* I was hooked — and had yet to discover the patron saint of the story of the opening of the American West, Bernard DeVoto, who won a 1947 Pulitzer for *Across the Wide Missouri.*

A.B. Guthrie lived in Choteau, Montana, on the eastern slope of the Rockies, which he called his "point of outlook on the universe." He also wrote the Academy Award-nominated screenplay for the movie *Shane.* His father was the first principal of the first high school in the Montana Territory.

Bernard DeVoto's *1846 — Year of Decision* is a delightfully told tracing of the many events in a pivotal year that molded so much of the West we know today: the Mormon pilgrimage, the annexation of Texas and a war with Mexico, the Donner Party, the Bear Flag Revolt, to name just a few. The definitive scholarly work for the period is *Exploration and Empire* by Yale professor William Goetzmann (Pulitzer, 1967). To complete this overlong bibliography, more recently Ivan Doig, William Kittredge, and Craig Johnson have captured the glory of Wyoming and Montana, as have latecomers to the region, Annie Proulx and James Lee Burke.

I am smitten, and was yet again on May 22nd and 23rd, on the road through the mountains and high plateaus of the West and toward home, still another twelve hundred miles away.

After the Devil's Tower detour in Wyoming, the next destination was Bozeman, Montana, a city just past the mid-point of that enormous state. Montana State University is in Bozeman, and restaurants and streets were filled with college students in graduation mode. Montana State entered the consciousness of many via Robert Pirsig's 1974 philosophical travel epic *Zen and the Art of Motorcycle Maintenance*. Aspiring writers may note that the book was rejected, famously, one-hundred and twenty-one times before it was published, has gone on to sell five million copies, and has never been out of print.

The college hoopla was refreshing to watch — enthusiasm, proud parents, undampened optimism, and overloud hijinks, none of which interrupted a good night's sleep after a long day. I was back on the road early the next morning.

Herewith, a geographical clarification: "The Rockies" does not refer to a mountain range, per se, as much as to the immense swath of territory that divides the North American continent north to south roughly along the 100th meridian — from British Columbia and Alberta to the Sangre de Cristo Range in New Mexico. The northern Rockies alone contain separate mountain ranges in their own right: the Bitterroots, the Absarokas, Sawtooths, Tobacco Roots, Bighorns, and many,

many more. From A.B. Guthrie's home in Choteau to Lander, Wyoming, takes eight hours alone, paralleling the eastern slope of the Rockies past Yellowstone, the Tetons, and the Wind River Range.

Several years ago, I decided to explore the state where the "river runs through it." From Sandpoint, Idaho, I drove east and stopped for the night and pitched my tent along the Clark Fork River. Three days later there still seemed no reason to pack up and move on. At breakfast each morning beside a campfire, I breathed in the aroma of rushing water, listened to woodpeckers knock on pine trees, and watched ospreys fish the river, elbows bent, "rowing through the air" (Brian Doyle, *Mink River*).

Since then, I've traveled the iconic expanse of mountains from Banff to Santa Fe, camping, hiking, taking photos and making notes. Before the Lewis and Clark bicentennial, Cherie and I traced the Corps of Discovery's trail from Great Falls to Lolo Pass with Stephen Ambrose's *Undaunted Courage* open in the car. At the Lewis and Clark Interpretive Center in Great Falls, Montana, we took turns pulling on a thick rope, trying to move a full-scale model of the impossibly heavy boats the men hauled up and over the now nonexistent falls. It wouldn't budge.

Out of Three Forks, Montana, we followed Meriwether Lewis's footsteps up the Jefferson River to the ridge at Lemhi Pass where he encountered a party of Shoshone and shared greetings. To his dismay, Lewis saw ahead of him not the Pacific Ocean he expected, but miles and miles of dark, formidable mountains fading into the distance.

By now my present-day narrative may have gushed too much and tried the reader's patience. But I have risked this digression to explain why, when I-90 picked up the Clark Fork River on the twenty-third day of this cross-country ramble, I gave a whoop. The next off-ramp led to a gravel road and down to the water's edge where I turned off the car and sat. The scenery was like a painting by Frederic Remington. Across the way, bright green trees glistened, backlit by distant snowy peaks. The river rushed by. An eagle soared. High up in a cottonwood tree, a pair of ospreys busied themselves with their outsized nest, an orderly mess of sticks and twigs.

Back on the highway, for miles and miles creeks rippled and cascaded and meandered through open expanses of land framed by multicolored buttes and cliffs. There were the usual crows and blackbirds and doves, but now more hawks and gulls, turkey vultures, and grazing antelope.

After awhile, downgrades began to outnumber the "ups" and the long, long descent into Coeur d'Alene began. Central Time had passed into Mountain Time, and Idaho gained me an additional hour. I stretched my legs at a rest stop, drank bad coffee, and chatted with the welcoming lady holding down a roadside Traveler's Friend kiosk.

The sun was well up in the western sky. If I made no stops and didn't encounter traffic, I could be home by 9:30 Pacific Daylight Time. I changed plans; I would push on and not spend the night in Spokane. One hand on the steering wheel, cruise-control set at 80, elbow resting on the window ledge and feeling the warm air of the Palouse, I set off to chase the sun, its rays scattering rainbows through gigantic irrigation sprinklers in Eastern Washington.

Had I really driven 7,000 miles? Visited twenty-three states (and the District of Columbia) in as many days? Friendly and pretty fellow passenger for much of the way?

A good time to reflect. What contrasts we had seen!

These days it's often hard to be optimistic about America. Rarely does a day go by without miserable newspaper headlines and TV film-at-eleven. It's all out there. You can't travel across the country and back and completely ignore that. We'd set out on a historical and a heritage exploration, not a social or political one, and a narrow, self-selected one at that. We hoped to sample flavors of America without, admittedly, digging too deeply into what they were about or why they got that way. It simply wasn't our focus — sort of like watching a movie without giving thought to the mechanics of the production or the backstage drama.

But consciousness and conscience were unavoidable. We saw scenes of poverty unlike those, sadly, we were used to at home: a shaggy person pushing a shopping cart full of black plastic bags, the mentally ill man gesticulating and talking to himself with no place to go, a woman holding a hand-drawn cardboard sign at an intersection, pleading.

Rural poverty was just as heart-wrenching. In southeast Colorado towns we passed unpainted and boarded-up buildings, faded for-sale signs, and idle people sitting out front, stuck in nowhere. Michael Harrington in *The Other America*, (1962) described poverty as a "separate culture, another nation, with its own way of life."

I thought of Woody Guthrie, too. In the Forties, reportedly he got tired hearing Kate Smith warble *God Bless America*, so he wrote his version of a national anthem.

> One bright sunny morning
> in the shadow of the steeple
> By the Relief Office
> I saw my people —

As they stood hungry,
I stood there wondering if
This land was made for you and me.

In Lamar, Colorado, census data reveals that one-third of the population is out of work, twice that of Colorado as a whole. Among teenagers and Latinos, the numbers are worse. In Las Animas, there is one blinking yellow stoplight left. Factories packed up and left. Fifty percent of the residents are below the poverty level, compared to seventeen percent in the rest of Colorado and fourteen percent in Washington. Yet there were Little League teams and swim meets and 4-H, diehards who refused to leave, and, a bachelorette party that made the local paper.

What we saw was a resolute "america" with a lower-case "a" — not indifferent, but "in spite of." An everyday, get-up-in-the-morning america; a sprawling, diverse country of 315 million people who don't make the news. Kids kicking soccer balls, dads shooting hoops in driveways with daughters, high school boys staring out classroom windows on sunny afternoons counting the hours until summer, a mom closing the office early to prepare for a church meeting that night, sisters and slumber parties, brothers wrestling on the lawn, old men telling lies on park benches, families with canoes on car roofs. And yes, tattoos on the arm of a pretty girl at her bachelorette party, her proud papa out front washing his pickup truck.

Our interactions were, in large part, with people in the hospitality industry — waitpersons, motel clerks, gas station attendants, shopkeepers. Did we understand that welcoming smiles might mask personal hardship, some of it tragic? To all of this, Yes. It's also entirely likely that conversation at a dinner table with someone we met along the way might make our mouths drop open; political and social and religious and awkwardly naïve opinions abound, of course. So does bigotry.

We didn't seek out nor did we ignore the blemishes; they are manifold, but that's another topic for another day.

It's a crazy-quilt, this sprawling country, but what to make of the craziness?

Insane drivers around Chicago and an obstinate turkey stopping traffic in Minnesota; the tale of a honeymooning pioneer woman who convalesced at a historic fort in the West after a miscarriage; a laid-back bait and tackle shop operator in the hills of Kentucky; a pretty, "gotcha covered" waitress at a crowded diner in a radar-blip of a town in the high Utah desert; crossing the Mississippi with an engaging scofflaw with a wandering eye and a pipe full of marijuana; a patient young woman in a toll booth at Mt. Rushmore. I appreciated the helpful fellow who shared with me the mystery of unlocking a stuck gas cap, as well as the chap in full regalia at Bent's Fort who shared his vast knowledge of the West. What a kind woman it was who bailed us out at a Sam's Club fuel pump plaza in Kansas.

Figures from the past, real and fictional, played a role: John C. Frémont, William Bent, Wyatt Earp, the Lone Ranger, Huck and Tom. So did folks who no one but their friends and relatives will likely remember. And poets: Woody Guthrie and A.B. Guthrie, meet Walt Whitman.

And vistas: eleven-thousand-foot Monarch Pass surrounded by peaks another four thousand feet higher, then down to flat-as-a-pancake Kansas where the horizon disappears and there are marshes and ponds full of exotic birds; the idyllic Blue Ridge Parkway and urban forests in Virginia; noisy traffic in downtown New York City where we sipped French roast coffee and overheard various spoken languages.

The feelings: the awestruck silence of open fields and desert viewed from an empty roadside, the frightening power of the Mississippi, the hours of mind-wandering driving, the warmth and smiling welcome from everyone we met along the way including, of course, family.

I have no no easy conclusion, no erudite finale to a journey, nearly one-thirtieth of the way to the moon, by the way. Just utter amazement at the length and breadth of the United States and the loose but strong fabric that holds its occupants together.

All of it almost makes no sense — other than the joy of opening our eyes to adventure and saying a profound thank-you. We'd do this again in a heartbeat.

* * * * *

I lost the race against the sun. It was dusk when I crossed Snoqualmie Pass. Luckily, Memorial Day weekend traffic was headed toward me *out of* Seattle.

I pulled into our driveway at 9:45. Home is good.

~ ~ ~ ~ ~ ~ ~

And the end of all our exploring
Will be to arrive where we started
And know the place for the first time.

*Little Gidding V*

T.S. Eliot

CPSIA information can be obtained
at www.ICGtesting.com
Printed in the USA
FSOW03n0054220716
22834FS